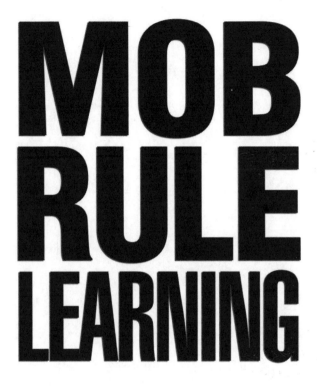

MOB
RULE
LEARNING

MOB RULE LEARNING

Camps, Unconferences, and Trashing the Talking Head

Michelle Boule

CyberAge Books

Medford, New Jersey

First Printing, 2011

Mob Rule Learning: Camp, Unconferences, and Trashing the Talking Head

Library of Congress Cataloging-in-Publication Data

Boule, Michelle, 1978-
  Mob rule learning : camps, unconferences, and trashing the talking head / Michelle Boule.
    p. cm.
  Includes index.
  ISBN-13: 978-0-910965-92-7 (pbk.)
  ISBN-10: 0-910965-92-7 ()
  1. Non-formal education. 2. Democracy and education. 3. Professional learning communities. 4. Congresses and conventions. I. Title.
  LC45.3.B68 2011
  371.04--dc23

                                                                2011026674
Printed and bound in the United States of America

President and CEO: Thomas H. Hogan, Sr.
Editor-in-Chief and Publisher: John B. Bryans
VP Graphics and Production: M. Heide Dengler
Managing Editor: Amy M. Reeve
Project Editor: Rachel Singer Gordon
Editorial Assistant: Brandi Scardilli
Book Designer: Kara Mia Jalkowski
Cover Designer: Lisa Conroy
Copyeditor: Pat Hadley-Miller
Proofreader: Sheryl A. McGrotty
Indexer: Candace Hyatt

www.infotoday.com

To Mr. Rochester,
who has always seen me as more than a plain Jane

I don't think we have any choice. I think we have an obligation to change the rules, to raise the bar, to play a different game, and to play it better than anyone has a right to believe possible.

—Seth Godin
Tribes: We Need You to Lead Us

CONTENTS

ACKNOWLEDGMENTS

There are many people who made this jaunt down the rabbit hole possible, and this is my opportunity to thank them. I know I will forget a lot of you, so please forgive me and consider yourself thanked. To librarians: I am so very proud to be in your ranks. You inspire me every day with your generosity and intelligence, and you work tirelessly behind the scenes to keep access to information open to all. If I listed all the librarians that had a hand in this book, I would have to list almost all the librarians I know. You guys are amazing. Thank you to everyone who put up with my big ideas and my big mouth, and gave me a chance anyway. I cannot tell Meredith Farkas, Jason Griffey, Paul Sharpe, and Karen Coombs thank you enough for being my frequent partners-in-crime, subverters-of-the-system, and a ton of fun over drinks. I have been blessed by my Tuesday night Bible study ladies for their prayers and encouragement as I tried to balance caring for a toddler and writing a book. Thanks to Kyle Jones, Michael Stephens, and the spring LIS 768 class for being wonderful. A humble thank you to Rachel Singer Gordon for pestering me, giving me the opportunity to write this book, and then editing it.

Anything of any great length that I write ends up with a theme song. It is something I latch onto early and then listen to over and over and over again as I write. For this book, it was the album *Edinburgh Toon* by the North Sea Gas. Those gentlemen do not know it, but I could not have written this without them. My family encouraged me through this process, and I am blessed by their love. Special thanks to Gideon, who almost always found "something else to do" while I was trying to write, despite his being less than 2 years old.

Last, but not least, a huge thank you to my husband, Ries, who believes in me, encourages me, and makes me laugh. I love all of you very much.

ABOUTTHEWEBSITE

www.wanderingeyre.com/mobrule

When dealing with technology, things change rapidly; new resources are always being developed, and discussions are happening all the time about camps, unconferences, and the changes in professional learning environments. Here are some suggestions to find the newest resources about the topics discussed in this book:

- For links to new tools, articles, and other information, visit the book's website at www.wanderingeyre.com/mobrule.

- Lengthy discussions of topics found in this book can occasionally be found on the author's website at www.wanderingeyre.com.

- To follow or participate in the discussion of the book on Twitter, follow the hashtag #mobrulelearning.

Disclaimer

Neither the publisher nor the author make any claim as to the results that may be obtained through the use of this webpage or of any of the internet resources it references or links to. Neither publisher nor author will be held liable for any results, or lack thereof, obtained by the use of this page or any of its links; for any third-party charges; or for any hardware, software, or other problems that may occur as the result of using it. This webpage is subject to change or discontinuation without notice at the discretion of the publisher and author.

PART ONE

And So It Begins ...

On October 10, 2003, something happened that fundamentally changed conferences. It changed the way conferences were organized, where conferences could happen, and the ways in which professionals share information with each other. This one event has had repercussions in how professional communities are created, how they grow, and how they are sustained. But this was such a small thing—just one guy trying to do something different.

Before October 10, 2003, the learning opportunities available to professionals were similar in that they all relied on the distribution of knowledge from one learned professional, "the talking head," to the masses. To be a talking head, one had to be vetted through a series of events, often involving publication in scholarly journals and speaking engagements on the accepted conference circuit. Talking heads were always successful and at the top of their professional game. In many professions, only information shared in accepted venues by accepted talking heads was considered valid to the industry. Information from the talking head was shared via conferences, professional and scholarly journals, in traditional classrooms (as professionals again sought out the halls of higher learning), and in the form of training offered by organizations and companies. Information was passed on to a passive learner from the talking head within these traditional models; no other options were sanctioned as valid.

Even before the unlikely event of 2003, the birth of the internet and its later influence into every corner of our lives gave individuals the ability to share, discover, and create information at an undreamed-of level. In the 1990s, the internet was one place that you could push information out to others. Websites became a new form of talking head. This was not a place for conversation—not yet. Nor was it a place for communities, although message boards provided an exception. Information was shared, but the internet had not yet reached its true potential to nurture vibrant communities.

Then, something truly amazing happened. The internet evolved into both a vehicle for pushing out information and a tool for creation. This has been called many things, including the Read-Write Web, the Remix Culture, and Web 2.0.[1] Whatever the phrase, this evolution meant that the internet suddenly gave people the ability not only to share information, but to create and connect in new ways. Communities on the web exploded with content created from original and remixed sources. People were able to share and learn things in new ways. It suddenly seemed that the possibilities were only as endless as our imaginations.

The internet, as we know it today, is a live thing with a life of its own, housing vibrant communities focused around almost any subject you can imagine—and a few you would never dream of. These communities are places that often start out as a useful tool, like photo sharing on Flickr (www.flickr.com), and evolve to become a place where people go to live, create, and interact with others—their third place. A person's third place is the place an individual goes to socialize and build community outside of home or work.[2] Social communities mean different things to different people and to different generations, but they are increasingly found in virtual spaces. This development of the virtual third place has seeped into our lives; the ubiquitous quality of the internet now means that our third places can also follow us anywhere—and they do. The lines between personal, professional, and social are becoming erased by the omnipresent nature of the web.

Communities on the internet do many things, but almost every community is about sharing something. People go online to share photos, share stories, give advice, seek advice, read, play games, find friends, find mates, create art, and do almost anything. But all of these communities create something, and increasingly that combination of information and creation means that people are creating their own learning communities. These communities share information among peers, be they mothers, teachers, librarians, photographers, or individuals editing the world's largest online encyclopedia, and all that shared knowledge means that these are also communities that learn from and teach each other.

We may not think of these as learning communities, because we tend to picture learning in a classroom, with a designated teacher and students paying rapt attention—but learning is happening. This ability for everyone to become simultaneously a teacher and a pupil has leveled the playing field. The internet has democratized learning. The power of the group has made itself known. The mob has created software, written encyclopedias, and discovered the human genome. The power of the mob is infinite because they will never run out of knowledge to share and things to explore. The mob can do anything.

This mob of creativity has begun to make itself known in professional arenas as well. We are no longer content to remain silent within our organizations. We no longer want to be simply cogs. We want to develop and contribute to the process. We want to serve each other by sharing the passions we hold dear. We want to build, create, and learn in new ways, and we do not want to fill out a form for permission. We are tired of talking heads with their big ideas. The mob has some ideas of their own.

On October 10, 2003, Tim O'Reilly decided to host a different kind of conference,[3] a conference where everyone was equal and everyone got to speak. He invited some innovative minds to come and share what they knew with others. The innovative minds were not talking heads; they were people doing some cool things with technology. O'Reilly thought he was just holding a gathering of smart, cool people, which would be named Foo Camp. But what he did was change the way we look at conferences and knowledge sharing, and the way we build professional communities. Foo Camp, the unconference that changed everything, resulted in a reconsideration of what conferences are for in the first place.

Conferences and other continuing education experiences should be about information and the community that grows from the experience of transferring that information. Instead, conferences and learning have become things that revolve around talking heads, the experts, and what they have to share. Community has been lost in the process. Thankfully, there is a movement afoot of people who are creating their own mobs outside of the accepted sphere of professional practice. These growing mobs are no longer content to be passive vessels, but are mobs that want to share and create the knowledge that they hold within. The mobs want to make their professions better, whatever that profession may be, and they are not going to ask permission from anyone.

This book is part history, part story and personal experience, part practical manual, and part manifesto. Ultimately, it is about how a mob of professionals can take the power back from the talking heads to educate themselves and share their collective knowledge in meaningful ways—and maybe, just maybe, change the world in the process.

Endnotes

1. Lawrence Lessig, *Remix: Making Art and Commerce Thrive in the Hybrid Economy* (New York: Penguin Press, 2008).

2. Ray Oldenburg, *The Great Good Place: Cafes, Coffee Shops, Bookstores, Bars, Hair Salons, and Other Hangouts at the Heart of a Community* (New York: De Capo Press, 1999).

3. "Welcome to Foo Camp," O'Reilly, wiki.oreillynet.com/foo-camp/index.cgi (accessed July 19, 2011).

CHAPTER ONE

Traditional Conferences:
What They Do and
How They Get It Wrong

Traditional conferences do have their place, and there are quite a few things that they get right. They serve an important role in the life of the professional and in the life of a professional organization. A traditional conference, for purposes of this discussion, is a face-to-face conference filled with scheduled sessions of speakers or panels that give a traditional long presentation followed by a question-and-answer period. Conferences are held by professional associations to educate members on new trends, offer networking opportunities, generate revenue for the organization, and bring members together to do the committee work of the organization.

Traditional Conferences Are Continuing Education

Other than professional and research journals, conferences are one of the more prominent ways that professionals continue their education as their career progresses. For those in academia, conference and paper presentations also help advance the road to tenure and gain professional pomp. These conferences are often the only way to gather points leading to tenure. People go to these conferences because they are expected to attend; this is part of an accepted process. Organizations often see conferences as a way to facilitate learning by bringing respected leaders in the field together in one location to discuss their current projects, interests, or topics. This facilitation of learning is one of the benefits of belonging to a large professional organization, and although members often pay to attend a conference separately from dues, conference learning is seen as a value-added service from organizations to their members. Many companies pay dues to professional organizations because it is seen as a necessity for the professional growth and development of their employees.

Traditional conferences bring together the dispersed members of an organization, which allows for diverse networking opportunities. Although there are many online social opportunities for almost any interest or profession, few things are better for cementing professional relationships than a happy hour with other conference attendees at the hotel bar or chatting after a session over coffee. The richness of these after-hour conversations led to the first iterations of an unconference ... but that story comes later.

Attending a conference organized by a major professional organization often affords a rare opportunity to hear the leaders in a field discuss important topics. The keynotes of big conferences are populated by speakers with big ideas and motivating words for the crowd. Large organizations can afford to pay the money required to have important or well-known talking heads as featured sessions, so this is one of the few places that regular members of a profession can gain access, however limited, to the prominent people in their field. Access is almost always set up in such a way that everyone knows who has the important idea, and who is supposed to listen to those ideas.

Traditional conferences do have many advantages over impromptu or online offerings, and this book does not argue that we should entirely do away with the traditional conference format (with which many of us have a love/hate relationship). The problem with most conferences, though, is that they have become more about the organization putting on the conference than the people attending the conference—the people who actually need information and networking opportunities. The best things about traditional conferences are the people who attend them, and this is often lost in a quagmire of bureaucracy, talking heads, and a sea of faces.

Traditional Conferences, Useful Information, and Learning

If the main objective of a conference is to present useful information to attendees and to facilitate learning, most conferences simply scrape by, and many fail outright. The knowledge that the general profession needs is not the knowledge that is frequently presented. Sessions at conferences are sometimes so specific as to be inapplicable in any other setting. These types of sessions frequently leave out the most important part of their message: how to repeat, scale, and improve on the idea in some other place or in answer to some tangential problem. The other most common type of session has similar problems, but for the opposite reason. This is the session that is so general as to be useless. These sessions may simply involve a rallying of the troops, but the lack of practical knowledge can be disheartening. The most useful learning, which occurs between professional peers, happens everywhere at a traditional conference except in the large presentation hall with rows of chairs and a projector screen. The most important learning and community building happens outside the conference session. Nothing can kill motivation and passion like a 300-person auditorium and a PowerPoint presentation.

Professionals may find that after all the money spent to attend a conference, after all the time spent sitting in uncomfortable chairs, and after all the hours listening to speakers drone on about things that are not as exciting as they appeared in the program, they learned the most from their peers in the hallway. This can be a bitter and expensive pill to swallow, especially if you are paying your own way. In academia, the jaded realize that many professionals go to conferences to present and check off boxes on their tenure track, not to listen to others, or even to learn at all. The more academic the conference, the more likely it will be that the speakers will be presenting on topics that are so specific that they are not applicable in any other setting. Seeing the work of others is interesting, but it is not always useful.

People attend conferences to find socialization and community, but community is not found in a lecture hall. Most professionals quickly learn that the best community at a conference is found in nonsanctioned activities, either online or at the bar. Like the meeting after the meeting in the workplace, the hotel bar and unplanned activities at conferences often yield the most networking opportunities. Backchannels contain better conversation than what is happening up on the stage, and you are free to ask any question that comes to mind—no microphone needed. (A *backchannel* is an online side conversation that occurs simultaneously during a conference session, class, or other gathering.) Maybe it is the relaxed atmosphere of these settings (or perhaps the drinks!), but some of the most fruitful and passionate ideas have been sketched on cocktail napkins. Not all cocktail napkin ideas will change the world, but feel free to dream. Every profession needs dreamers.

Conferences are often seen as a way to network with other people interested in the same niches of the profession, but other than exchanging business cards, there are rarely built-in mechanisms for continuing relationships after the conference is over. Attendees may use informal methods of keeping in touch in online venues, but these spaces are not sponsored by or directly related to the conference. They might read each other's blogs or follow each other on Twitter (www.twitter.com), for example. Many tools, though, could easily be implemented to provide an online venue for sharing conference information and as a place to continue relationships begun at a conference.

Wikis, forums, social networks, and photo sharing sites all provide a free way for conferences to add spaces for interaction and community building. These tools are not new, but traditional conferences have been slow to adopt and adapt them for their members—so members often take matters into their own hands and create these spaces themselves. A traditional conference could use online spaces not only as venues for continued conversation, but as a method of marketing as well.

At a large conference, the levels among attendees, speakers, and conference-planning groups are legion. Conferences are frequently planned either by members of the profession who have already reached the echelon of management or tenure, or by their secretaries, who may or may not have a good working knowledge of the profession itself. It is not that managers do not have relevant and important knowledge, but they do sometimes lack practical knowledge. This is especially true of managers for whom their position removes them, physically and organizationally, from the people carrying out the everyday activity of the profession. Speakers tend to be experienced leaders in the field. This often translates into management, and for many speakers it has been a long time since they placed a foot behind a service point, classroom, or lab. In academia, this can be compounded by speakers who have only research knowledge but no practical experience in the real world. Conference attendees, on the other hand, are those getting their hands dirty on the frontlines and behind the lab bench. The needs and experiences of conference attendees and planners vary widely, and it is hard to believe that many planners know or remember what it was like to be a simple cog in the machine.

This distance between attendee and planner or speaker results in some other unfortunate consequences. The conference planners may not actually know what the lower levels of the profession need to know. What problems does the profession currently face on a micro level? This separation of planners and attendees means that there is often a lack of practical and directly applicable information. At the conclusion of the conference, attendees seldom come away with actions to take home that will make the individual or the organization to which they belong better. Outside of gatherings of IT- or technology-oriented professionals, there is likely a huge technology gap and a gap in expectations within the profession as well. Greener members of the profession may expect things like free wireless, while many more seasoned members would not see the lack of wireless as a disaster of the largest proportions. Can you really have a conference without wireless internet access? The answer is yes, but I do not think a highly successful conference can be fabulous without one.

There are many ways that presentations go wrong at conferences. A presentation by a professional talking head may be inspirational, containing dreams, fluffy clouds, and bunnies, or it may be a dire forecasting if the profession does not change the world—yesterday! These two presentation types serve a purpose. They do motivate us to be better, stronger, and dream larger, but they do not give most professionals tools to accomplish this world takeover. Even worse are presentations to an audience of trench workers given by a management type who has forgotten what it was like to work with the public 20 years ago. Then, there are always the presentations that go bad due to the speakers' inabilities or to an unskilled use of PowerPoint, but these trends are not particular to traditional conferences and can sadly be found in almost any venue, anywhere, at any time. Unfortunately, in a traditional conference, attendees do not know how bad the presentation will be until it starts, and then it is difficult, if not impossible, to escape unnoticed. You, and 300 other sorry souls, are stuck for the next couple of hours in an uncomfortable chair, learning nothing.

The larger the conference, the more unlikely it is that the specific needs of individuals will be met. One person may be facing a particular research issue they need help solving and another individual may be looking for a way to create a new tiered level of company service. It is improbable that the scheduled sessions and keynotes will specifically address these particular challenges. Addressing specific challenges is not the purpose of a large conference, but they can be solved in a small gathering of one's peers with a more informal structure—at an unconference, perhaps. (We'll talk more in depth about unconferences throughout, but for now, an *unconference* is a gathering of people interested in a topic or idea, with no preset schedule or structure. The structure and schedule is determined by the participants on the day of the event.)

The conference-planning process bears some responsibility for the lack of timeliness and applicable presentations at a conference. Many conference programs are planned six months to a year or more in advance, because venues and big-name talking heads must be scheduled, programs must be printed, and advertising for potential attendees and vendors must be sent out. The problem is that in an age when timeliness is defined by technology and the internet, six months, a year, or beyond is far too long for a conference topic to be gathering dust. A conference topic submitted a year or more in advance will be woefully outdated by the time it sees a conference stage. An antiquated conference session, planned a year ago, does little good and certainly does not advance the understanding of the individual or the profession.

Conferences and the Internet

The internet has made new information available at a rate that has all but rendered the traditional conference presentation and the print journal (to say nothing of the scholarly book) useless. (This book has its own timeliness issues as well, so for updated information please visit the companion website at www.wanderingeyre.com/mobrule.) Professionals conducting research, writing down the next big idea for a profession, or simply discussing developments, can do it all quickly on the internet. Online journals, blogs, and even Twitter offer a quick way to push information to others with similar interests.

Communities like Twitter and Facebook (www.facebook.com) can be used to query professional colleagues when you face a particularly puzzling problem. No longer must a good idea go through a laborious print-vetting process, involving months of writing, editing, submitting, more editing, and finally publication of research conducted a year or more ago that is no longer relevant. The vetting process in the online community is quicker, faster, and more transparent.

A traditional conference, even of modest proportions, involves a large overhead of time, money, and space. Conference planning takes time to organize, and this negatively impacts the timeliness of the information presented. At a traditional conference, there are sessions to vet, programs and official schedules to print, rooms to set up in specific ways, and big-name talking heads to pay or convince to address your group. All of these things take significant amounts of both time and money.

Vetting the sessions and getting print materials together for a conference of any size is a large undertaking, and many organizations do this work by committee. Most vetting processes take time, and this is one of the reasons that papers and program proposals are requested months to a year or more in advance. Shuffling all those papers back and forth is always a lengthy process.

The size of an organization and its conferences is directly proportional to the amount of time and overhead needed to schedule the space to house all the members of a group once they descend upon a city. The American Library Association (ALA) holds one of the largest professional conferences, with an annual attendance of around 28,000 people, and tends to take over almost every large hotel in the host city during the conference.[1] It is staggering to think that some person is responsible for making sure that Room 237 in Hotel X has its chairs in the proper formation and the right signage is placed by the door. The time needed and expended on a conference this size is so great as to be prohibitive. There is almost no way a conference of 28,000 people can be reactive, or better, proactive, in seeking out timely information for attendees. Because of its size, ALA is limited to the cities that can hold that many bibliophiles descending in the span of a few days. ALA accomplishes this feat of scheduling with full-time staff and multiple divisions that are responsible for planning their own activities and meetings. Large conferences also cost more money; all of the planning, printing, space, and big-name speakers can require significant funding. Again, the size of the traditional conference is proportional to the money and hours spent on planning it.

Conference printing and work can result in a significant amount of waste. As soon as the conference is over (and occasionally before), all of the programs, flyers, and handouts go into the nearest trash bin. Paper cups, cans, and water bottles join the paper trash. Some conferences have tried to combat paper trash by putting programs and speaker handouts on preloaded USB drives, asking attendees to bring and reuse their own water bottles, or having recycling bins in the conference area. Some larger conferences have even begun to take notice of the food waste generated during meetings and programs. Green conferences are starting to gain more support and ground across industries, but waste continues to be a major issue at traditional conferences and business meetings.

Access to information about a conference, its sessions, handouts, video, audio, or other generated material is often limited because of usability issues or because the sponsoring organization has hidden the information behind a wall. There are various reasons and methodologies for keeping conference information behind a wall, but most of them have to do with money and access. Plenty of organizations believe that if they give conference information away for free, especially when it comes to session and event content, then people would never pay to attend a physical conference. This belief belies the real benefit that professionals reap when attending a physical conference, namely, meeting peers in informal settings, coffee breaks, and happy hours, and making important connections for future projects and research. A few organizations charge a reduced rate for synchronous online conference events, giving access to information with some added webcasts thrown in.

Conference websites can also be irritating to navigate if they are not easily searchable. Some websites are merely place holders for the venue information and do not contain session information at all. Other websites created for conferences have places for all of these things, but everything is hidden behind a wall. Sometimes a peek over the wall costs extra money, even if you *did* attend the physical event. Other times, attendees of the physical event will be given full access to this information, as long as they create and remember an account for the conference webpage.

The best systems for recording and storing this type of information are open, allow access without a wall, and can easily be edited at least by the speakers—and ideally by the attendees as well. The speakers can add links to handouts and slides, and the participants can add links to session summaries. The obvious example would be using a wiki for this type of information gathering. Some large conferences have begun adding official wikis to their conference information sites, but these types of community-building practices are still not the norm.

A Problem of Scale

All the challenges and issues that traditional conferences face can be reduced down to a problem of scale. As planners are further removed from the attendees, and as the number of attendees increases, it is less and less likely that any given individual will have his or her needs met. Traditional conferences are not where niche needs are met, and we do not normally expect them to be—but why not? Why couldn't we turn conferences into the long tail of professional gatherings? Chris Anderson argues that niches, not large blockbusters, are what will drive the future of business. This theory of the Long Tail, or the idea that the majority of the market can be served—and in fact, desires—small niche products that serve specific needs, can be applied beautifully to conferences.[2] If the needs of individuals are niches on the tail of conferences, then unconferences may be the answer to filling the niches. A small gathering of people, self-organizing, has a greater potential to meet their own needs. If individuals participate with passion in an unconference, they will have opportunities to share that passion and their ideas with others. At a small gathering, an individual is more likely to be able to convey the current challenge he or she is facing. Placing the challenge into a gathering of peers means that the challenge then has the opportunity to be addressed, sometimes even solved, by the gathering. Then the individuals can take that knowledge with them and use it to impact their professions, their organizations, the world, or possibly all three. This is what unconferences can do. Unconferences fill the niches in our professional gatherings. They make it possible to share the kind of passion that makes it impossible to leave the event without feeling like you are able to change the world. Our larger conferences have lost this ability of impact.

And is that not what all of us want? To change the world and make it better?

Endnotes

1. "American Library Association Conferences and Exhibitions," American Library Association, exhibitors.ala.org (accessed July 19, 2011).
2. Chris Anderson, *The Long Tail: Why the Future of Business Is Selling Less of More, Revised and Updated* (New York: Hyperion, 2008), Kindle ebook.

CHAPTER TWO

(Un)Defining a Camp or Unconference

A camp or unconference (the terms are used interchangeably here) is a conference exemplified by its distinct lack of structure. From the outside, an unconference may at times appear to be chaos in motion, but it is this distinct lack of structure that makes an unconference both a novel experience and a success. This chapter explains some of the origins and elements of the unconference.

Open Space Technology

To truly understand why unconferences work, when everything we are taught to expect from a conference says they should fail, we have to take a small detour to look at a concept known as Open Space Technology (OST). This is not a technology in the traditional sense, but rather in the anthropological sense. In anthropology, a technology is anything that changes the way a society behaves, constructs, or is structured. Examples of technology under this definition would be flint knapping, weaving, democracy, or the internet. OST is a belief system that has changed the way some people approach meetings of all kinds. It hinges on the belief that a group of people, given a purpose and freedom, have the ability to self-govern, self-organize, and produce results. A meeting or conference using OST will have little or no agenda, no predetermined outcomes, and no predetermined leaders. Individuals gather together with an idea and then are set free. This freedom can often produce unexpected and wonderful results.

In 1983, Harrison Owen spent a year toiling to plan a conference. Like many conferences, most of the participants agreed it had been great, but what everyone loved the most were the coffee breaks.[1] Like the hotel bar, the coffee break area can often yield not only the best connections, but the best conversations. According to the OST website, "In Open Space meetings, events and organizations, participants create and manage their own agenda of parallel working sessions around a central theme of strategic importance."[2] OST can be used for any gathering of people, from five to 2,000-plus, to accomplish anything from goal setting, a traditional weekly meeting, or a conference. Owen says that OST works because it is based on "passion bounded by responsibility."[3] People participate and share because they are passionate about something, but they move into action, or walk toward a solution, because of responsibility.

The main concept and principle of OST is open communication among people. Many things in the OST methodology have been given representative shapes, and Owen talks about OST being a circle.[4] The way a room is set up for a meeting tells the participants everything they need to know about who holds the authority and who does not. In a class or large conference room, the chairs are in rows and they all face the front, the place of authority, and the talking head. In a circle, all are equal. With no head and no sides, everyone has the same authority and right to participate. Circles, asserts Owen, "create communication."[5]

The idea of open communication is important, and it is one of the concepts that define a well-run mob learning experience. At a traditional conference, open communication is rarely encouraged or allowed, from the way proposals are submitted to facilitation styles. In fact, almost everything about a traditional conference precludes the sharing of opinions by the masses. Sessions may have a Q&A period at the end, but speakers frequently talk into this allotted time for the audience. At a traditional conference, you have attendees, not participants. Attendees simply attend. They are expected to listen, absorb, think; they are not expected to actively participate in the agenda, the topics, the discussion, or their learning. At a gathering governed by OST, all people at the event are expected to participate in meaningful ways. Participants at an unconference are rarely idle, physically or mentally.

The flow of OST, the sequence of events, follows four ideas: the marketplace, the bulletin board, the circle, and breathing. When participants arrive, they spend the first hour placing ideas and concepts into the marketplace. Ideas are written onto cards and posted or written on a board in a central area. This identifies ideas and topics in which people are interested. Participants then indicate through a number of different ways (e.g., multivoting, discussed later in this chapter) which ideas are the most important to the group as a whole. This information can be used to create an agenda, program, or schedule of events. The third sequence, the circle, involves open communication and sharing, sitting in a circle and discussing the topic at hand. As previously stated, circles are important to reinforce the idea that all participants and ideas are of equal value and that all are expected to engage in the process.

Breathing, the last sequence of events in the flow of OST, is also an important concept that makes OST so successful. Breathing means that when you need to leave a discussion, session, or workshop to clear your head, to relax, or to cool off during a particularly heated discussion, you are encouraged to do so. After breathing and clearing your head, you are then free to join the session you left or find somewhere else you would rather be. This is strongly related to the Law of Two Feet. The Law of Two feet is simply the idea that people can and should use their feet to vote for what is most interesting and engaging to them. (For further discussion of The Law of

Two Feet, see Chapter 3.) Getting up, moving about, and changing your perception are tenets of OST. The idea that participants take time to breathe and then consider the ideas being shared is another way that OST reinforces the idea that, though others may have different opinions or needs than your own, they have a right to share them. Encouraging participants to leave when they need to means that fewer arguments erupt and that participants can leave to find the place where they are best engaged.

There are four rules or principles that govern OST gatherings. These rules are not meant to bind, but to set free. These four principles are:

1. Whoever comes is the right people.

2. Whatever happens is the only thing that could have.

3. When it starts is the right time.

4. When it's over, it's over.[6]

"Whoever comes is the right people" means that the people who show up to participate are the people that are supposed to be there, the people with the necessary passion. After the people show up, the sequence of events that follow is the only thing that could have happened in that time and space. This frees the gathering from a predecided agenda or program, because the participants are determining the events instead of the event determining the event. It seems like common sense that people should be able to choose the topics that speak to them directly instead of this being decided for them. The third principle may be the hardest for most people to understand, and that is the idea that time, as we know it, does not matter much. Things go on as long as they need to until they are finished and then, they are done. This fluid idea of time goes directly against the idea of a conference schedule. The last concept speaks to the finality of the events and a peace with the process. When it is over, there are no thoughts of what might have been. The event is concluded, and people must accept the events as they occurred, not wish for something different.

This concept of whoever comes is the right people also means that whatever number of people you have, large or small, is a workable group for discussion, learning, and creating. Many unconferences do tend to be smaller gatherings, running at fewer than 100 attendees, because the concept is new and few people know what to expect. People tend to avoid the unknown. Topics also tend to be more focused and less broad than in larger, more established conferences. The OST website says that this idea of self-organization can scale up to 2,000-plus people, though there are no examples of this on the site. An unconference of that size would require some facilitation to help people get started and organized; a large group would likely create many smaller discussion groups and have more ideas to sort through, especially at the beginning. This kind of scale is fine, but the facilitator must allow for more time during the initial discussion periods in which the group decides on topics.

The four principles mean freedom. Freed from making certain that the "right people"—those with accepted authority and the talking heads—make an appearance, facilitators and participants are free to learn and share what they know. Freed from an agenda and schedule, the event can unfold to address and meet the needs of the people attending, not the needs of the talking heads to hear themselves or of the academics seeking an audience for their ideas. Freed from time, anything can happen. Freed from regrets, participants can move on to the work at hand that inevitably comes from a productive learning session with peers. Often this work is the work of people who want to make a difference, to change the world.

This idea of freedom at a conference rubs most of us the wrong way. As humans we strive to control that which we do not understand—or that which is generally out of our ability to control in the first place. This is one of the reasons why wars are waged and hatred nurtured. Control is what the idea of OST fights against. If given enough freedom, any group of people will self-organize into a structured system. This has been a truism for OST from the beginning. Owen states that "the only way to bring an Open Space gathering to its knees is to attempt to control it."[7] Superimposing a structure onto OST causes it to fail.

The OST website is replete with examples of groups that "should" have gathered and accomplished absolutely nothing but frustration—and an agenda for yet more fruitless meetings. However, using OST, they not only worked together, but at the end of just days (not months or years) they had a plan, a written version of the plan, and action items in hand. In one of the examples, a failing cellular phone company met to determine its future. Amazingly, the people who stepped forward to save the company, the people with all the ideas, "came from the trenches."[8] It is not only remarkable that the leadership came from the lowest rungs in the corporate ladder, but that the management allowed them to take the reins. As stated before, this lack of control is what allows OST to flourish and be successful. Flexibility and open communication result in more ideas being shared by more people.

Owen does have one caution for people considering using OST for a gathering: Groups with a long previous history have more trouble self-organizing because they tend to fall back into comfortable and accepted roles.[9] A meeting between people who have worked closely together in the past may find it hard to self-organize, because in their minds they already see certain people as the leaders and others as the followers. OST can still work for groups like this, but facilitators and planners should be aware of this phenomenon.

The concept that drives OST from chaos to success is "passion bounded by responsibility."[10] Passion gets people involved in the process and responsibility moves them to get involved in finding the solution to the problem at hand. People attend conferences because they are interested, often passionately, about the topic at hand. Asking that much passion to sit passively in a conference session is a waste of time, energy, and possibility. If you instead give participants an actual say in how their learning and sharing occurs, there is no end to the possibilities.

Though OST is not common vernacular, even among people who frequently attend unconferences, it is easy to see how the free-flowing, self-organizing conference owes its roots to Harrison Owen's idea. Unconferences have many things in common with the OST ideals.

Common Unconference Elements

The main element of an unconference that makes it differ from a traditional conference is its schedule—or rather, the lack of an official schedule. There are a few different ways to create a schedule for an unconference, and the method you choose will greatly depend on your audience, and perhaps even the sponsor of your gathering. First, the schedule can be voted on by the participants in advance, letting the participants both suggest the topics and then vote on the ones that should be featured. Second, the schedule can be decided through various facilitation styles (some are discussed later) on the day of the actual conference. Using this method, there is generally a broad theme for the camp, but specific topics are suggested and chosen the day of the conference. Third, some combination of preplanning and day-of-the-event planning is used. A combination of planned and spontaneous schedule creation is useful when either the sponsor or the participants are particularly uncomfortable or unfamiliar with a completely unscripted event.

Traditional conferences are built around the talking head, the glorified expert, but at an unconference, everyone has, and is expected, to contribute his or her area of expertise. An accepted truth at most unconferences is that everyone has something to contribute because everyone is an expert at something or has some inside knowledge that no one else can share. The planning, facilitation, and follow-through of an unconference are all built around peer sharing.

Educational research has shown that students learn better when they actively participate and when they have the opportunity to teach others.[11] Though this is a common practice in K–12 and higher education, we often forget to apply this when we are adults, learning and gathering for professional reasons.

As discussed in Chapter 1, many traditional conferences and professional organizations tend to be large, while most unconferences and camps tend to be small. The combination of self-organization and smaller groups at unconferences allows participants to make better connections with each other and take more of a leadership role in the proceedings. At unconferences every participant is encouraged and expected to actively participate by presenting, facilitating, or contributing to the discussions. In a larger, traditional group, these kinds of participatory expectations are often not realistic or encouraged. Time and anonymity are the main enemies of larger traditional conferences. At an unconference, time and size are less meaningful.

The size of a traditional organization or event is directly proportional to the layers of nuance, red tape, and money spent on archiving and sharing the proceedings. I have seen professional organizations create large online structures for sharing conference proceedings that they then charge people ridiculous amounts of money to access. Access to the information is often restricted and hard to share outside of those who have paid to use it. In order to create this monstrosity of a web portal, or whatever catchy name is being used, there were probably at least two committees involved, hours of bickering, and countless time spent making every entry just right. Sadly, much of the time and money spent on official proceedings could have been better spent elsewhere. There are too many tools available and too many people willing to pitch in for proceedings to be anything but cheap and simple.

At an unconference, the archiving, discussion, and occasional work that is done after an event happens organically as a result of the event itself. At many OST gatherings, the proceedings and action items are typed and printed for every participant before the event is concluded. Many camps and unconferences are organized around a wiki or other website that allows a democratic sharing and editing process to take place. This is a natural place for people to put links, have discussions, and continue work that began at the unconference. Happily, a wiki or other tool, in addition to acting as an organic discussion and planning device, works great for archiving as well.

At an unconference there is often no distinction between social time and learning time. The informal nature of many unconference facilitation styles allows participants to be relaxed, to share, and to learn. As previously stated, participants are expected to actively participate in an unconference. In this exercise, they are invariably sharing part of themselves with others, whether through well-spoken discussion or lighthearted banter. Sharing time is learning time. Ultimately, this is the goal of an unconference—sharing and learning.

An unconference is unscripted, unscheduled, and unpredictable. This does not mean that an unconference is an unfacilitated event. Mobs may have a purpose and a goal, but someone needs to point them in the right direction. In *Crowdsourcing*, Jeff Howe talks about the need for a benevolent dictatorship.[12] Howe asserts that no matter how smart the crowd, there must be some kind of facilitation. The benevolent dictator is a leader who is led by the needs of the group rather than personal politics. Of course, leadership and guidance are needed to make an unconference successful, but the hand is usually light. David Snowden, quoted by Don Tapscott, says that the best leaders are like kindergarten teachers: "Experienced teachers allow a degree of freedom at the start of a session, then intervene to stabilize desirable patterns and destabilize undesirable ones ... And when they are very clever, they seed the space so that the patterns they want are more likely to emerge."[13] Snowden could be describing an unconference or any gathering of people left to self-organize. Although some intervention may be necessary to keep the process going, most groups will organically move forward as different leaders step up at the precise time they are needed.

In fact, one of the amazing things about unconferences is that they allow people who previously did not have leadership roles to step up and lead. Seth Godin defines this choice to step up and be a leader as "the choice to not do nothing."[14] At an unconference, people are there because they care and they lead because they have something to contribute. They contribute the passion they brought with them to the process of learning, sharing, and problem solving. For most of us, the structure in which we work and how we interact within that structure (e.g., our companies, universities, and organizations) also governs how we work and interact with people. Removing people from these known structures removes people from the need to defer to accepted leaders, opening up the stage for new leaders to step forward. As discussed earlier in this chapter, Harrison Owen has found that groups with a rigid structure using self-organizing methods of facilitation for a gathering will find it difficult to break out of their mold.

Facilitation Styles

Talking heads and talking head panels rarely appear at an unconference. There are, however, some different yet effective facilitation styles that show up during unconferences, and there are many choices and styles from which to choose. A good unconference should seek to combine a number of these styles so that people with different comfort levels and learning styles will be engaged. Because many of the attendees may be unfamiliar with the different facilitation styles used at unconferences, it is important to spend some time at the beginning explaining the methods to the participants. Allow for some discussion and questions of the technique itself if needed. Facilitation styles can be chosen before the event, during the event, or a combination of both. The styles chosen should reflect the topic of the gathering and the participants. The process of choosing a facilitation style is discussed in Chapter 4, which covers how to plan a successful camp. The rest of this chapter is not meant to be an exhaustive list, but rather a guide to some of the common facilitation styles used at unconferences.

Appreciative inquiry is a facilitation method commonly used for groups needing organizational change. It can, however, be an interesting method to use as part of an unconference schedule. When discussing a topic, appreciative inquiry focuses on what works, instead of the areas of a topic that fail or are problematic. There are four steps to the process: Discovery, Dream, Design, and Destiny.[15] In the Discovery step, the group lists the things that work. Next, the group Dreams of what could happen if the things that work well are allowed to reach their peak. Third, the group Designs a plan to make their dreams a reality. Last, the group executes the Destiny they have planned. For instance, if the discussion topic is "Facebook Usage During the Workday," appreciative inquiry would seek ways that Facebook benefits the workday. Then the group members would envision how these benefits could be used in the long run; they create a plan to make their dreams a reality, and they work toward that goal.

Appreciative inquiry would be useful at an unconference if you were seeking to take participants from a challenging topic to an action group. For an unconference that wants the participants to leave with actions in hand, an agenda to change the world for the greater good, this might be an interesting style to employ.

Birds of a Feather is a common name for a meeting in which a group gathers to discuss a general topic, idea, or question. Once in the group, there is no agenda or schedule, just an open discussion that weaves to and fro as the group wishes. The only structure for this type of meeting is that there should be an agreed-on time for the discussion to conclude. There is often a group facilitator to make sure that the discussion moves along and that no one person dominates the group.

Dotmocracy (www.dotmocracy.org), also called the multivoting method, is democracy and idea sharing in its purest form. There are many different ways to facilitate a Dotmocracy or a multivote, but Dotmocracy is an official technique with its own handbook. In the multivote format, the group brainstorms on a topic or question. Solutions are placed on large sheets of paper around the room, on tables, on a whiteboard, or in some other prominent place. After all ideas are documented, on sheets of paper or whatever is being used, members get three to five colorful dot stickers or small sticky notes to vote for their favorite ideas. Participants can use their votes however they choose, by using all their votes on one idea, using no votes at all, or placing them on different ideas. The votes are then tallied, and the ideas with the most votes are the winners. This is a great way to choose topics for discussion at a conference or as a way of setting an agenda at any meeting.

The official Dotmocracy method uses the same concepts as out-lined in the multivote method, but there are official ideas, voting sheets, and a handbook that you can download from the Dotmocracy website. Unlike a multivote, which is anonymous, a Dotmocracy vote involves signing your name to your vote (see Figure 2.1). After all the voting is concluded in a Dotmocracy, a "trusted decision maker" chooses from the most popular ideas and makes the final decision about what the group will do.

The Fishbowl method is named for the way in which the chairs are set up, with a small circle of four to six chairs in the middle of a larger circle of chairs. In the smaller, inner circle, one of the chairs is left blank and the other chairs are filled. The rest of the members fill the outer circle. A facilitator poses the question or topic to the group and the inner circle starts discussing the issue. The outer circle, or audience, listens to the discussion happening in the fishbowl, the middle circle. When a member of the audience has something to add to the discussion, that person joins the fishbowl by sitting in the empty chair. At this point, one of the participants of the fishbowl

Figure 2.1

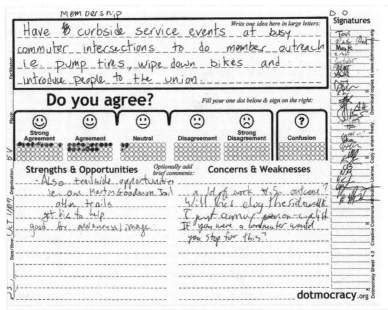

On the official Dotmocracy sheet, there is a space for the idea to be written, discussed, and voted on. This sheet was filled in at BikeCamp09 in Toronto, Canada. (Photo by Jason Diceman of www.dotmocracy.org)

must voluntarily leave so that there is always an empty chair in the middle. The discussion continues until the time limit is reached.

Introductions and getting to know other participants is part of the excitement of an unconference, so this activity should be facilitated in a fun way. Participants can give tagged introductions where they are asked to stand up, say their name and give two tags that describe themselves, but no other information. You can also do a version of speed dating, where participants have 10 minutes to meet 10 new people and exchange business cards. Be creative. Make meeting new people a game instead of a task.

The *Knowledge Cafe* is a two-tiered discussion method that is interesting because of its lack of reporting from smaller groups to a larger discussion group. In this method, the entire group of attendees gathers to hear the topic and one or two key questions to lead the discussion. For example, the topic may be ebooks as a format, and the questions may be, "How will ebooks change the way libraries, bookstores, and publishing companies do business?" and "How does copyright or Digital Rights Management as we know it today support, encourage, or hinder the ebook format?" After hearing the topic and questions, the large group breaks into smaller groups of about five people to discuss the questions.

The small groups meet for about 45 minutes. No notes or records of the discussion are taken for official reporting. At the end of the period, all the groups meet again in a large discussion area. The large group then spends some time discussing the questions. Participants do not report what their groups discussed, but instead bring up ideas that were discussed in the natural flow of the larger group conversation. The large group discussion should flow from the discussion that occurred in the smaller groups, not be a rehashing of the smaller group discussions. Again, no recording is done of the large group discussion for record keeping. The facilitator should make sure that one person does not dominate the discussion.

Lightning Talks (also known as *Speed Geeking* or *Dork Shorts*) are similar to the idea of speed dating. In a large room, a handful of presenters set up round tables with a circle of chairs around them. Each presenter has a small audience, which listens and asks questions of them as time permits. At the end of a short period of time, usually 10 minutes or less, the facilitator ends the discussion and the audience rotates to the next speaker. There are a few alternative versions of this. The speaker can move instead of the audience, which cuts down on the time in between sessions, as five people moving is less chaotic than 200 people shifting around a room. You can also have the groups be fluid, allowing the audience to join and leave groups at will. Although this is more flexible to the audience, it can be frustrating for presenters as information often needs to be repeated as new people arrive. In this last variation involving free movement within groups, there would be no change period, just, for example, 45 minutes in which the audience could float among five groups.

Nominal Group Technique, similar to multivoting, allows every participant to offer a topic (or solution if used organizationally) to the unconference schedule and then allows the group to decide, by voting, which topics will be presented. There are a few different ways to complete the voting. Voting can occur during the unconference or it can take place before the unconference begins. Once all topics have been presented, duplicates are eliminated. The participants then rank the topics, assigning numbers to their top three or up to top 10 choices. The number of choices will vary depending on time and space restrictions. The numbers each topic receives are totaled. Topics with the lowest score are ranked higher than those with larger scores. This ranked list of topics can then be used to create a schedule of popular topics at the unconference for presentations, discussions, or workshops.

Open Space Technology, as discussed earlier in the chapter, is a facilitation style in which the group is left to self organize. Participants are gathered together under a common topic and then left to decide the agenda, schedule, and action items (if any) that come from the gathering. OST works with groups of five to 2,000 members. The group should be given a time limit, often one hour, in which to create a schedule for the day.

PechaKucha and *Ignite* are both trademarked names for a presentation style that involves showing PowerPoint slides very briefly during a short presentation. PechaKucha was created by two architects from Tokyo, Mark Dytham and Astrid Klein. At a PechaKucha event, a speaker shows 20 slides for 20 seconds each, making the entire presentation 6 minutes and 40 seconds long.[16] The first PechaKucha event was held in Tokyo in 2003, but today there are events all over the world. Ignite is a similar idea, started in Seattle by Brady Forrest and Bre Pettis in 2006.[17] In the Ignite format, 20 slides are shown for 15 seconds each, for an entire time limit of 5 minutes. Limiting the speaking time and PowerPoint usage of presenters means that more people can present than at a traditional conference and presenters are forced to be creative with their small time frame.

There are many facilitation styles, not discussed here, that can easily be adapted to an unconference environment. A mob that chooses the method with which they will interact will be a mob that is engaged in the process just as much as in the content. A facilitator should always leave flexibility in the schedule for the group to choose different styles. Experiment with greeting styles as well and allow the participants time to get to know each other in unique ways. When exploring new facilitation methods for an unconference, the most important things to remember when planning a successful event are transparency and sharing. Be willing to experiment, and remember that whatever happens was the thing that was supposed to happen.

Endnotes

1. Harrison Owen, Introduction to *Open Space Technology: A User's Guide* (1992), www.openspaceworld.org/cgi/wiki.cgi?InTheBeginning (accessed July 19, 2011).

2. Michael Herman, "What is Open Space Technology?" Open Space World, www.openspaceworld.org/cgi/wiki.cgi?AboutOpenSpace (accessed July 19, 2011).

3. Michael Herman, "Open Space Explanations," Open Space World, www.open spaceworld.org/cgi/wiki.cgi?OpenSpaceExplanations (accessed July 19, 2011).

4. Harrison Owen, Introduction *to Open Space Technology.*

5. Ibid.

6. Michael Herman, "Open Space Explanations."

7. Harrison Owen, "Emerging Order in Open Space," Open Space World, www.openspaceworld.org/cgi/wiki.cgi?EmergingOrderInOpenSpace (accessed July 19, 2011).

8. Harrison Owen, Introduction to *Open Space Technology.*

9. Harrison Owen, "Emerging Order in Open Space."

10. Michael Herman, "Open Space Explanations."

11. Barbara Leigh Smith and Jean T. MacGregor, "What Is Collaborative Learning?" Washington Center for Improving the Quality of Undergraduate Education (1992), learningcommons.evergreen.edu/pdf/collab.pdf (accessed July 19, 2011).

12. Jeff Howe, *Crowdsourcing: Why the Power of the Crowd Is Driving the Future of Business* (New York: Crown Business, 2008): 284.

13. Don Tapscott and Anthony D. Williams, *Wikinomics: How Mass Collaboration Changes Everything* (New York: Portfolio, 2008), Kindle ebook: location 6101–6105.

14. Seth Godin, *Tribes: We Need You to Lead Us* (New York: Portfolio, 2008): 59.

15. Richard Seel, "Appreciative Inquiry," New Paradigm, www.new-paradigm.co.uk/Appreciative.htm (accessed July 19, 2011).

16. "PechaKucha 20x20," Klein Dytham Architecture, www.pecha-kucha.org (accessed July 19, 2011).

17. Ignite, O'Reilly Media, ignite.oreilly.com (accessed July 19, 2011).

CHAPTER THREE

The Good, the Bad, and the Unscripted

Unconferences are unscripted, unplanned, off-the-cuff, exciting, fun, chaotic, immediate, and largely an unknown—though this, too, is transitory. The idea of the unconference, though these have been held in different forms since the 1980s, is relatively new to most people. Outside of the technology-related professions, unconferences and camps are a rare phenomenon. Trying to explain the amorphous nature of an unconference is like predicting the trajectory of a herd of cats. It is confusing and frustrating, and leaves you wondering why anyone would herd cats in the first place. But, this amorphous nature is what makes an unconference so successful. The form can adapt to the group, the goal, the setting, the time, and the technology. Transparency and flexibility craft amazing results when wielded by a passionate group—although this flexibility can also be its Achilles Heel.

Benefits of an Unconference

The most important advantage to an unconference, making it far superior to a traditional conference, is the time involved in planning the actual event. A traditional conference involves countless people, committees, and a year or more of planning time, while an unconference can easily be planned in a few weeks. This short planning time means that an unconference also requires fewer people to organize and execute. The hardest parts of planning an unconference are securing a venue and making sure the technology available is appropriate for the topic. Time is not an obstacle for unconferences.

Time is important to many fields, especially when a technology-related theme is involved, and the ability to quickly plan a conference can be crucial to the applicability of the ideas shared. A conference with even the most shallow of technology topics will be irrelevant if the topics were chosen and vetted a year before the actual event; technology evolves too fast for a year-old topic to be cutting edge. Unconferences, with their short planning time, can easily accommodate topics that have emerged up to a few weeks before the event. The planning period for an unconference is short because the attendees do most of the topic planning themselves, relieving the facilitators from choosing what they believe to be the most pressing topics. Participants can choose the topics before the unconference event, or topics can be chosen the first day of the gathering. Relevancy is rarely an issue given these circumstances because the participants are choosing what is most relevant to them.

If a traditional conference is looking for ways to add both immediacy and relevancy, an unconference can easily be tacked onto it. An unconference can be added almost anywhere in a traditional conference schedule. A full- or half-day preconference session can give a traditional conference momentum at the beginning by setting a tone of collaboration, energy, and innovation. At the end of a conference, an unconference can be a great collaborative way for attendees to synthesize new information and share practical applications of what was learned. Immediacy, missing in traditional conferences, is always an element of unconferences—because topics, schedules, and discussions spring from the minds of the participants in that moment. Participants bring to the group their current knowledge, questions, and solutions in ways that a traditional session, planned and written by a talking head months in advance, cannot. Realize, though, that an unconference that must compete against traditional programming in the schedule may be avoided by attendees because it is largely an unknown concept. Given a choice, people tend to gravitate toward what they know.

An unconference event at a traditional conference has the added benefit of getting attendees actively involved in their conference experience, simply by the nature of how unconferences work. Active participants in an event feel much more invested than attendees who sit and passively listen for hours. Participation is the second most important key to unconferences. In fact, without participation, unconferences would not exist. Their nature hinges on it. They work because people come to share, and they come to share because they are passionate about the subject. The people who come want to contribute. They want to be there. They want to learn. They want to use their passion to change their organization, their community, or the world. Unconferences allow people to engage in a process that places them on the road to changing their surroundings with their passion.

At an unconference, the power and decisions over content, schedule, and outcomes are firmly in the hands of the participants. Most traditional conferences determine content, schedule, and outcomes with various committees and review boards. At a traditional conference, decisions about who will present on what topics at a particular time and in a specific room occur far removed from the people who will be attending the conference session. Although the topic may be interesting to the 10 people planning the conference, it may not appeal to the thousands who will gather in a year to hear the talking head. Giving the decision-making power to the participants allows them to decide what they are there to learn and share. They will choose the things that are most immediate to their needs, things they are invested in, and things that they will not only stay around to hear, but to which they will actively contribute.

Unconferences demand participation. Participants are not often allowed, by the very structure of the gathering, to be passive. There are few audiences at unconferences—and even fewer talking heads. For some unconferences, BarCamp being the primary example, the simple act of signing up to attend the conference is a process that requires you to state how you will contribute to the day. (BarCamp, an unconference after which many others are patterned, is discussed in more detail as a case study in Chapter 5.) At BarCamp, when you place your name on the list of attendees, you have to state what topic you are interested in and if you are willing to present on that topic or another topic in which you have some expertise. People attending their first BarCamp are strongly encouraged—one might even use the word *required*—to present. At other unconferences, when you sign your name to attend you have to choose if you are willing to present or facilitate a discussion. There is no choice for passive listening. It may be harder to be passive at an unconference than it is to participate at a traditional conference.

Unconferences involve active learning. The more ways we can manipulate new information, through seeing, listening, trial and error, or peer instruction, the better we can understand and apply that information. This is why in school you had to do homework, practice problems, work in chemistry labs, and complete science projects. It is why plays are read out loud in English class. We make better sense of things that we experience, not just things we observe.[1] Passive learning is not the kind of learning that changes your understanding, and unconferences are active learning in motion. At an unconference, people can present an idea, participate in a discussion, vote on the topics of the day, and teach others—and they can also choose to leave something that is not meeting their needs. The process of learning does not stop when the event is over. Participants of unconferences are encouraged to apply their new knowledge to impact their profession, community, or world.

At any gathering, people are almost always free to get up and leave the room, but at an unconference people are *encouraged* to leave when the discussion is not meeting their needs or to take a break. In Open Space Technology, this is called the Law of Two Feet (see Chapter 2).[2] If, at any time, a participant is not learning from the proceedings or contributing in some way, they are encouraged to leave that group and join another. This has also been called voting with your feet. If a topic is not engaging or interesting, people will simply leave and there will be no more audience for the speaker or group for discussion. From a presenter or facilitator's viewpoint, this also means that all of the people left in the audience or group will be engaged in the conversation. Only people who are contributing to the process stay, which means the discussion will continue to evolve in a healthy and diverse manner. In a traditional gathering, leaving in the middle of a discussion or session can be downright rude or interruptive. At an unconference, this is a natural process, which allows the most important topics to come to the top of the heap and be addressed directly. The topics and discussions that are the most important, the ones in which people can participate in the most, and the ones in which people are learning, are given the opportunity to grow and expand. In some cases, simply giving people a choice will assure that they stay longer in one place. The knowledge that they have an option, some freedom, may give people an incentive to stay and be involved.

The Law of Two Feet, in addition to allowing people to leave a session that is not engaging, gives participants permission to leave a conversation that has become too heated or heavy. At an unconference, the people gathered are often passionate about the topic they are sharing with others, and this can occasionally lead to clashes in both personalities and ideas. This will be especially true when this self-organizing style is used for meetings, planning groups, and other working groups. The greater the diversity of the group and the larger variety of ideas gathered, the greater the chance there may be conflict. At an unconference, people becoming too heated to contribute productively are encouraged to leave the discussion for a time to cool off. Participants can use the time away to reflect on the discussion without the influence of others. This helps avoid large-scale arguments, as people who have time to reflect on the discussion can often rejoin a group and be productive instead of argumentative. Quiet time may give them space to reformulate their argument or consider the ideas of others in a new light. Leaving a discussion can simply give people time to decompress the ideas shared. Some people learn better after time and reflection are given to a topic, so being able to leave a session for a few minutes of quiet contemplation allows these participants to rejoin the discussion renewed and better able to contribute. The simple act of getting up and moving around also contributes to people's ability to learn, because movement means that the participant is not asleep. (Sitting too long can cause an almost sleep-like state, especially given a boring speaker and a warm room!) Unconferences are anything but a passive learning environment.

An unconference can be created with a schedule including diverse facilitation types so that many different learning styles are met. While not the main purpose of employing various styles, this is one of the results. Different styles will engage different people, and one person's favorite discussion style is another's nightmare. If participants have a hand in choosing the schedule, they will choose facilitation styles that match their own learning styles. Even participants who may not know their exact learning style will often gravitate to sessions in which they are most comfortable. Purposely planning an unconference schedule with a variety of facilitation styles and presentation types gives the gathering a diversity that not only meets different learning need but is also engaging. At a traditional conference, the sameness of the presentations is mind numbing—a talking head, a large room, a large audience, and a boring PowerPoint presentation. Diversity in presentation styles can engage the minds of participants through the simple means of changing the known.

Though not always the case, unconferences tend to be smaller gatherings than traditional conferences. Lower numbers of attendees means that sessions are smaller, and the types of facilitation styles used at unconferences frequently are geared to smaller groups. In a smaller group, it is more likely that an individual is able to participate and learn. There is less competition for time in the discussion, and individuals who are uncomfortable sharing may be more apt to do so in a smaller group. Smaller groups also develop a sense of camaraderie early on that is missing from larger, lecture-style gatherings. Simply choosing to be part of a small group helps you to identify, and later share, with the crowd.

New leaders can emerge when groups are given the opportunity to self-organize. If traditional roles are left behind and the groups are small, individuals who had previously not been given either the opportunity to share their opinions or to act as leaders will come forward. New leaders or emerging leaders are sometimes intimidated by the old guard. An unconference, with its lack of structure, can ease some of the tension that people on the lower rungs feel when stepping up in a public forum. Sometimes, this is just the push or forum that a new leader needs. When gatekeepers and talking heads are abandoned, new people in the field can share their expertise. We all have an area of expertise and knowledge to share; all that we require is a forum. Fostering emerging leaders means fostering new ideas, new innovations, and new directions. Unconferences give new ideas and leaders a forum by removing barriers to discussion and knowledge sharing.

The informal nature of an unconference results in a gathering in which people are more likely to be honest and openly share knowledge. The feudal systems of most conferences ensure that the peasants stay peasants and that those in power keep their manors by limiting participation from the masses. There is only so much power that can be wrested away by an audience at a traditional conference—and the more successful methods may get you thrown out. An unconference, though, is a gathering of peers who have similar goals, challenges, and ideas. An unconference is not populated by talking heads, gatekeepers, and the masses beneath them. It is easier to be open with people you perceive as your equals, and an unconference is a level playing field of knowledge in which all have the right and responsibility to contribute.

Money, an issue that seems to always crop up, gives unconferences a huge advantage in contrast to traditional conferences. Due to its informal structure and nature, an unconference can be planned and executed for little to no money; donations and sponsors can easily supply what is needed. Unconferences, planned by the masses and not a committee or executive board, have little overhead. The highest costs at any unconference are the venue and the technology (mainly internet access for the event itself). Most unconferences find a venue as cheaply as possible, many finding a space that can be donated to the event. Unconferences do often have a large population of participants who are technologically savvy, and the nature of the way information is often shared during unconferences, via wikis, blogs, and backchannels, means that internet access for all attendees is a need, not a want.

Internet access also gives these events the potential to generate some interesting conversations during the unconference with people who are not physically attending. If the purpose of your event is to influence your profession, impact your community, or change the world, then spreading knowledge to as many people as possible is a good thing. Participants with internet access can post their reflections, conversations, and action items in real time.

Holding an unconference at a traditional conference center or hotel, which charges astronomical prices for internet access, can in many cases be counterproductive. One of the benefits of unconferences is their cheap operating price, and paying for a traditional venue defeats that purpose. Many cities have technology centers that are available to groups for reduced rates, and most libraries have facilities that will accommodate an unconference gathering. If the group is small, even a private location with wireless could serve the purpose. The first Foo Camp was held at O'Reilly's media office in Sebastopol, California, with people camping out.[3] An unconference does not have to be fancy; it just has to have space for the gathering of people and ideas. The people who attend, not the facility, talking heads, or food, are what give an unconference meaning.

Unconferences can be planned by a small number of people in a short amount of time. The more planning power that is placed in the hands of the participants, the less planning the planning group must undertake. Organizing an unconference mostly involves finding a venue with internet access and marketing the event. Booking a venue can be done in a single day, and marketing can be as simple as placing some well-worded blurbs on some social networking sites. A technology unconference that is planned mere weeks before the gathering is sure to be cutting edge and involve topics on the cusp of development.

Unconferences also fail to generate the same large volume of waste as a traditional conference. An unconference does not usually have a printed schedule, program, or handouts. Unconferences are frequently planned on wikis because of the democratic nature of the way in which people are able to participate in a wiki space. A wiki can be used for the schedule planning, as a gathering of session material, a listing of participants and their contact information, and as a FAQ for the venue or unconference. Putting all of this information on a wiki not only gathers it into one place, but it means that little of it will likely be printed out onto paper. Less paper means less waste, and a smaller group means less waste. At Foo Camp, the original unconference, participants camp out and bring their own towels. There is no hotel waste at Foo Camp, because there is no hotel. Foo Camp is one of the case studies in Chapter 5.

Unconferences rely on chaos to thrive and succeed, and because of this they do have limitations and drawbacks. Most of the problems that arise in planning and executing an unconference revolve around the challenge of managing the chaos of the mob. The mob and their informal nature, an unconference's greatest assets, are also its greatest liabilities.

Common Challenges With Unconferences

Jeff Howe refers to the ability of the mob to break down as the "dumbness of crowds."[4] Without a direction, goal, or purpose, a mob can easily break down and become just a group of people standing around. Common wisdom would have us believe that any group is only as strong as its weakest link. James Surowiecki argues that the group is always smarter than the individual, given the chance to make independent decisions.[5] The collective knowledge of the crowd is always greater than the knowledge of one learned individual. Tapscott and Williams say that it is the mob's ability to drive the knowledge economy, an ability they call wikinomics, which overcomes the weakest denominator.[6] All of these authors believe in the truism that the average belief or educated guess of the mob will always be closer to the truth or reveal the actual truth of the problem with more efficiency and accuracy than the guess of the individual. However, without some direction, a topic on which to focus, or a methodology for discussion, the chaos of the mob can overrule their ability to be useful. Any group of people from disparate backgrounds can lose track of their initial goal and focus.

Howe argues in *Crowdsourcing* that a "benevolent dictator" is needed to overcome the ability of the mob to lose focus and thus effectiveness.[7] As previously discussed, a self-organized gathering like an unconference gives new and emerging leaders the ability to step up and stretch their wings. If a leader does not step up, though, the mob may be left without clear direction. A facilitator can give the mob direction by guiding the mob through decision making with a facilitation method. A self-organizing group will need a leader if there is no facilitator. Without a leader, you have a mob doing nothing in particular, or at least nothing useful.

The leader who steps forward will need to be a "benevolent dictator": Someone who can guide but not interfere.[8] If the leader is too domineering or overbearing, that person can block the work of the group. A good facilitator should keep an eye out for this kind of railroading. In the ideal scenario, the group itself will regulate the authoritarian leader by producing an alternative facilitator or by simply staging a coup. The Chinese philosopher Lao-tzu states that the ideal leader "is best when people barely know that he exists, not so good when people obey and acclaim him; worse when they despise him."[9] An unconference can lose focus and direction if the leaders who emerge are focused on their individual goals and not on the goals of the group and the topic at hand.

Groups that are very large may have trouble scaling the unconference concept to fit their needs. Open Source Technology (OST) says that it can be scaled to fit any group, but there is some point at which the chaos becomes too unruly. Some professional organizations are too large to attempt an unconference for their entire membership. The American Library Association (ALA), for instance, which recently boasted an annual conference attendance of almost 29,000 people, could not realistically plan an unconference of this size. Divisions within ALA do plan their own smaller unconference gatherings as a way to incorporate this informal idea sharing into the larger conference structure. There is no conclusive evidence on what size is too large, but OST insists that allowing self-organization works with five to 2,000-plus people.[10]

The flexibility that comes with relying on the chaos of the crowd to solve problems and for the crowd to learn from each other also makes this method hard to explain and understand. Trying to define an unconference is like trying to explain the shape of clouds. A cloud rarely remains still for long, shifting and floating with the air and changing shapes. The structure of a self-organized group has the ability of a cloud to change and move. This serves the group well when it needs to change direction or reorder the flow of work in order to better learn, share, and solve the problem before it. The structural force of an unconference may be the topic to be discussed; it might be the structure around which the mob chooses facilitation styles and subtopics. In a society that has spent much of life structured and ordered, leaving important learning and work to the winds of change can seem foolhardy. The amazing thing about crowds is that they seem to always evolve and come out on top.

Unconferences are like snowflakes, each as unique as the people attending. The knowledge of the individual, shared with the mob, is what adds depth and structure to the group. The lack of a uniform structure also can be an invalidating force to gatekeepers and those in power within an organization. This problem of a lack of clear definition for an unconference makes the process hard to explain to people in power—the Powers That Be (PTBs)—from whom you need permission or funding to hold your event. Unfortunately, we must sometimes seek the blessings of those in power and we need to be able to explain this chaos that we would like to harness for learning. PTBs and gatekeepers are often loath to support what they do not understand, and they are even more reluctant to commit money to something as metamorphic as a crowd. Most managers and PTBs want some assurance that the money given will be invested with a sure rate of return. An unconference, as unstructured and unexplainable as it is, assures one of nothing so much as that people will gather and learn … something. This can be a hard sell, especially for managers used to authoritarian rule and an organization that is not used to transparency.

Authoritarian professions that have very structured methods for professional learning will find unconferences may be hard to adopt as an acceptable method for sharing official knowledge. Academia, for instance, is built upon the succession of writing, presenting, and learning from only accepted gatekeeping bodies in the field on one's road to tenure. These kinds of rigid learning and knowledge-sharing structures both have the most to gain and the most to fear from the ideas at unconferences. Giving the power of learning back to the crowd will result in many gatekeepers being out of a job. Gatekeeping bodies may fear that proper vetting of research and ideas will not occur in a mob atmosphere, but the opposite is actually true. A crowd that has its own identity, Wikipedia (www.wikipedia.org), for example, does an excellent job of vetting its own information. If a random coterie of people on the internet can build an encyclopedia that rivals its printed cousins, why can't a face-to-face gathering of researchers in a field vet each other's ideas and knowledge?

Unconferences and camps as a concept can easily be applied to many different kinds of gatherings, including working groups within organizations, staff training, project and strategic planning, and group problem solving. At its heart, an unconference involves the sharing of ideas and knowledge, whatever form that knowledge may take and within whatever structure that knowledge might reside. People in power are unlikely to be comfortable with allowing a group to self-organize when their task is something as important as strategic planning. Mob rule, when allowed to thrive, can produce some amazing results, but the mob must be allowed to work as a mob. That kind of release of power and trust goes against the grain of most organizations and managers. The idea of using this unconference structure for other tasks is further discussed in Chapter 6.

The mob, and the power and weakness of unconferences, can be overcome with good leaders when proper scaling is accomplished. The cons of an unconference, when given benevolent leadership, a clear facilitation style, and a dynamic topic about which the participants are passionate can be turned into pros with benefits that far outweigh the risks. People fear the unknown, and unconferences are clearly an unknown because of their unscripted nature. Learning always means trying new things. The unknown can be a place of fear, but it does not have to be. We never learn without taking a leap. Experiencing the amazing energy and passion of an unconference is a thrilling leap to take.

Endnotes

1. Michael Prince, "Does Active Learning Work? A Review of the Research," *Journal of Engineering Education* 93, no. 3 (2004): 223–231, www4.ncsu.edu/unity/lockers/users/f/felder/public/Papers/Prince_AL.pdf (accessed July 19, 2011).

2. Harrison Owen, "Emerging Order in Open Space," Open Space World, www.openspaceworld.org/cgi/wiki.cgi?EmergingOrderInOpenSpace (accessed July 19, 2011).

3. "Welcome to Foo Camp," O'Reilly Media, wiki.oreillynet.com/foo-camp/index.cgi (accessed July 19, 2011).

4. Jeff Howe, *Crowdsourcing: Why the Power of the Crowd Is Driving the Future of Business* (New York: Crown Business, 2008): 284.

5. James Surowiecki, *The Wisdom of Crowds* (New York: Anchor, 2005), Kindle ebook: Location 72–73.

6. Don Tapscott and Anthony D. Williams, *Wikinomics: How Mass Collaboration Changes Everything* (New York: Portfolio, 2008), Kindle ebook.

7. Jeff Howe, *Crowdsourcing*.

8. Ibid.

9. Ori Brafman and Rod A. Beckstrom, *The Starfish and the Spider: The Unstoppable Power of Leaderless Organizations* (New York: Portfolio, 2006): 114.

10. Open Space World, www.openspaceworld.org (accessed July 19, 2011).

CHAPTER FOUR

How to Plan and Execute
a Successful Camp

Unconferences may be the result of mob rule and chaos, but they do require some planning and facilitation. A well-run unconference does not, as previously discussed, require a host of committees and hundreds of hours to plan; one can be planned by two or more people with the help of the mob and some well-chosen technology.

The planning timeline for an unconference can vary widely. Some unconferences, like Mashup Camp (discussed in Chapter 5), are planned from idea to execution in less than 2 months. The first BarCamp, also discussed in Chapter 5, was planned in less than a week. Most unconferences can easily be planned in 2 to 3 months. The following is a simplified timeline (more details follow later in the chapter).

1 year to 2 months before the event:

- Form the Planning Group (PG), which usually ranges from two to five people and will handle the process of creating the unconference.

- Decide what the topic of the unconference will be. (This often happens organically as the PG forms. A group of like-minded individuals decide they would like to gather other individuals together to discuss and learn about a topic, and thus an unconference is born.)

- Find a location for the event and decide if there will be a cap on the attendance numbers. This may be dictated by the facility used for the day of the event or it may be governed by the size of the gathering the PG wants to host. The larger the mob, the greater the diversity of opinion, but a larger group also produces more chaos.

- Decide what kind of facilitation style will be used for the unconference. Will the participants decide the schedule, presentation or facilitation styles, and topics? Will some aspects be decided beforehand?

- Create a time limit. How long does the PG want the unconference to last? A day? Two days? As long as it takes?

- Make arrangements for lodging if the unconference is going to last longer than a day. Offer some housing options to participants.

- Decide what kind of refreshments will be needed for the event (drinks, snacks, lunch, and so on).

- Look for sponsors if the PG needs to raise funds for the event. For example, participants can be asked to donate funds for food.

1–2 months before the event:

- Advertise the unconference in every place applicable: on lists, blogs, Twitter, and Facebook, and through professional organizations. Online word of mouth is the way that most unconferences are announced.

- Engage in guerrilla marketing. If this is being held in conjunction with another professional conference, you can hand out flyers at that event, have people who are seen often at the conference wear a T-shirt or button advertising your unconference, or be creative and do something unexpected. A flash mob unconference perhaps? Even if your participant list is full, encourage others to follow and participate in the conversations online.

- Communicate the schedule and planning process to the participant list (the people who will be coming to the unconference). Let them know what will be available in terms of technology (wireless, power strips, etc.) and if there are lunch plans. People like to be prepared, so give participants as much information as possible.

- Create a tentative schedule by deciding what kind of presentations and groups you will have and how long they will last. If you are setting the schedule completely beforehand, you can use an online voting system with which participants can choose the topics for the presentations and groups. You may choose to have only part of the schedule set before the event, allowing for some flexibility; or you may have a blank slate, allowing the participants to decide everything during the first hour or two of the unconference. Whatever the PG decides, the participants should be kept well informed of the plans.

- Collect the swag for your event. If you are distributing any T-shirts, USB drives, mugs, and so on, now is the time to order those shiny giveaways.

- Gather a few volunteers in addition to the PG. Volunteers can help with people-wrangling on the day of the event. They are essential to running a smooth unconference.

1–2 weeks before the event:

- Print or provide name tags.

- Gather the supplies needed: power strips, flip charts, markers, blank paper, pens, projectors, laptops, and so on.

- Double-check the venue, food order (if you have one), and any other last minute supply runs.

The day of the unconference:

- Make sure that all participants know their jobs, and then let the mob loose.

- Build in a few minutes before different events to explain the procedure if there are some people new to the unconference style or if you are planning some new facilitation styles. Make sure that volunteers are on hand during schedule shifts to answer questions.

- Have fun!

Planning the Plan

The most important element in planning an unconference is keeping your audience in mind. Often, the profession, purpose of the camp, and the level of technological knowledge will guide the decisions about planning, venue, and technology needed for the event. If your target participants are not often first adopters of technology, you may not want to rely completely on cutting-edge technology for organization and archiving. If your profession does not deal well with slightly controlled chaos, a completely open schedule may not be the wisest way to introduce them to unconferences. Often, an organization can have a successful unconference event by planning some things in advance, but leaving room for the participants to add to the schedule. The following sections discuss options for planning, marketing, gathering, and archiving the event. All of your choices will have everything to do with the intended audience. Never, ever choose a technology because it is cool or looks fun. Define the need and then choose an appropriate (and occasionally cool) technology to solve your challenge.

It might be worthwhile to remember the Powers That Be (PTBs) from which you need to gain approval for your event. If you do not need approval or are planning to subvert the approval system (always a fun option), then you are lucky, daring, or both. If the PTBs are not your intended audience and they are not inclined either toward things they do not understand, or chaos, you may need to tone down those aspects for them. You could also give your PTBs an "Unconferences 101" information session to ease the way. Ideally, you are searching for a happy medium if you need to go through gatekeepers of any kind.

After you decide on the topic or focus of your unconference, the next step is to find a physical venue. Booking the venue is one of the few things that needs to be done a couple of months to a year in advance. When looking for a space, remember four things: cost, accessibility, size, and technology.

Cost can be crippling if you have a small or nonexistent budget. If this is the case, though, you still have some good options:

- Libraries often have rooms available to the public, and you can usually reserve them for free. Many libraries have wireless internet available as well, solving another issue.

- Larger cities may have a technology center that offers classes or rooms that could be used for an unconference. (If the technology center helps sponsor the event, it may be willing to give you the space for a small fee.)

- Community centers may also work, if they have the required technology.

- A company with large meeting rooms could be willing to open their doors in exchange for sponsorship and marketing. It never hurts to ask.

- Local colleges, universities, or community colleges may also have space available for reservation by the public at little or no cost. Some colleges may require that the space be reserved by an employee or student—in this case, find an ally on campus. They may have other resources you need, including technology, volunteers, and/or marketing.

If cost is not an issue, then you can reserve space at a traditional facility, like a hotel or conference center. These venues tend to be costly choices—not necessarily in terms of the physical space, but in terms of the technology for the event. For most gatherings now, internet access is imperative. This can be pricey at traditional venues, ranging up to thousands of dollars for one internet connection, and much more if you want open wireless access. Although wireless internet access should not be that expensive, when booking at a traditional facility you're at their technological mercy. Be aware of these issues and be honest with your technology needs when booking your venue.

Accessibility of the venue and nearby amenities should be considered, especially if you anticipate out-of-town attendees. Is the venue on a well-run bus route? Is there a train station close by? Is it easy to find by car? Is there parking available? If you are not providing lunch, are there places to eat nearby? All of these issues should be considered when choosing a physical space for your unconference gathering. Do not forget to provide maps, links, and transportation information on the unconference website. You could also try putting a little faith in your mob by putting up the space for the information and then letting the locals fill in the gaps.

The facilitation style you choose will impact the kind of physical space you will need. If you plan on spending all your time in a large group, then one large room with flexible seating and tables that can be moved will be perfect. If you plan on breaking out into groups, you will need a venue with both a large room and several smaller, breakout rooms. The seating in all of the rooms should be as flexible as possible, allowing the participants to move furniture around as needed depending on the groupings they choose. Unconferences are all about flexibility, and the physical space should support that as much as possible. You can use a large room for breakouts, but it is easier to do breakouts in separate smaller rooms. If you only have one large space, though, you can simply move chairs to different areas of the room.

Small unconferences allow for both flexibility and intimacy. One of the first things a planner will have to decide is if, and to what extent, to limit attendance. Keeping attendance less than 300 is common, and for some unconferences the number is quite small, less than 100. The physical venue may dictate the number of participants, or you may want to limit the participants based on the type of facilitation style you would like to employ. Decisions on attendance boundaries are best made early so that when you announce the event you have an idea about when and if you need to cap registration. Having a general idea about the number of people you want to attend will help you plan for not only the physical space, but also any extra volunteers needed for people-wrangling on the day of the actual event. For a 100-person event, a small planning group plus three to four volunteers is ideal. This gives you enough help to wrangle people during the day, hand out name tags or swag, and assist participants with the technology.

The last thing to consider when choosing a venue is that technology, for both presenters (if you have them) and for participants. If you are going to have some traditional, talking-head presentations, then you will need a room with some sort of projection system, a sound system for larger groups, and internet access for the presenter. Even if you are choosing one of the more dynamic presentation styles, like PechaKucha or Lightning Talks, you will likely need, at the very least, a projection system and internet access. If presenters will not have internet access, they should be told as soon as possible. Later in this chapter, we will talk about open communication during the planning process.

Again, internet access for all is essential for the success of most unconferences. An informal poll of participants at the American Library Association's first unconference in 2009 showed that they would have preferred open wireless to being fed lunch. For a room of bibliophiles, internet access was more important than eating. Participants want internet access for many reasons, most of which will benefit your event. Participants with internet access will blog, tweet, Facebook, post photos, and chat their way through your unconference. These social networks serve as an informal archive of your event, spread the word of what participants are learning to other people with similar interests, and give you insight as to how your event impacted your professional community. In some cases, the learning that occurs during the event will continue in online venues through connections made during the unconference. People have come to expect wireless access, and its lack will be a serious blow to the success of your gathering. Even if you are using the unconference format for staff training or project planning, internet access gives participants the option of using online tools that could greatly enhance the outcome of the group. If nothing else, the internet access gives participants the opportunity to participate in a backchannel during the event.

Unconferences are not about technology, but technology often harnesses some of the chaos into something great. The technology needs of an unconference occur in three phases: the planning and registration phase, the event phase, and the archiving phase. Each need requires different aspects of the tools you choose and, though there may be a single tool that can meet all of your needs, a combination of tools with one central hub is often ideal. Again, keep in mind your audience's technological experience and the sophistication of the tools you are considering. An unconference is not made by technology, and depending on your target group, the least technology-heavy option may be the most desirable. This next section will discuss the kinds of tools available. Remember when choosing tools that your participants will be diverse both geographically and in terms of their technological skill. Technology tools will be discussed in general terms; for a complete list of specific tools and further resources, please see the Appendix or the book's website at wanderingeyre. com/mobrule.

Unconferences are built on the idea that people are smart enough both to self-organize and to self-educate. This stems from a belief in transparency, in communication, in work, and in outcomes. The technology you choose to facilitate your unconference, or the lack thereof, should always be made in a spirit of openness. The choices and the reasons they are made should be made in such a way that every participant, should they choose, knows the reasoning behind the choices made. The participants should also feel able to discuss these choices openly with the organizers and with fellow participants. In addition to applying this transparency to the act of choosing tools, the tools themselves should foster transparency and sharing. It is folly to require your participants to give up the rights to the content they create. For example, never set up a system to archive presentations at your unconference that requires participants to hand over rights to their work to you. It is acceptable, though, to require that participants make their work available in such a way that it can be shared with others attending the conference. Asking participants to post their presentations and pictures under a Creative Commons (www.creativecommons.org) license is a great way for creators to retain the rights of attribution while allowing people to use the content. A Creative Commons license allows creators to place a copyright on their work, digital or physical, which allows or restricts a variety of uses, including remixing, sharing, attribution, and commercial use.

The main tool for sharing, be it a wiki, blog, content management system, or something else, should also allow people other than editors to contribute. Information hidden behind walls will not benefit anyone; information wants to be free and transparent. An unconference is not just a one-day event; it is about building communities of like-minded people. (For a great example of how an unconference can become an ongoing community force, see the PodCamp case study in Chapter 5.) A technology that requires users to give up more than they would receive in using it, or asks them to jump through hoops, will result sometimes in public revolt by your participants. Keep transparency a goal in all phases of your unconference and allow participants to contribute, which will help prevent ill will and bad press. Most misunderstandings and challenges can be fixed with open conversations and the willingness to be flexible.

Any style of unconference has some planning and registration technology requirements. Choose a tool with which you can both plan and register people to help simplify the steps and time you and the other participants will spend on this phase of the unconference. The main site for the unconference should have flexibility, the ability to pull in RSS feeds from outside sources, the ability to allow users (however you designate or regulate that) to contribute content, and should not require much technology knowledge to use.

The obvious, most simple, and cheap or free choice for these needs is a wiki. Nothing beats it for price and short learning curve. A wiki can be used to discuss and archive ideas, and provide a central URL, as a place to keep registration; it has the ability to be edited by many users and can be used as an archiving tool later. Wikis come in myriad flavors and many of them are open source, free, or very cheap. Most wikis have a discussion feature for particular pages, and this can be used as a discussion area for planning, and later for participants. Because a wiki is an open collaboration tool, its use philosophy fits nicely with the self-organizing, democratic mentality of most unconferences. A wiki allows the participants to decide how and what to place on the unconference's web presence. A wiki also can provide a place to centralize links to other information and products of the unconference, including links to reports, videos, and other discussions. With some manipulation, widgets of RSS feeds from outside sources or group chat rooms can be embedded into the wiki itself.

Wikis are not perfect. They will require some administrative attention, especially if you use password protection or require your participants to register in some way. Administering a wiki is as simple as keeping a friendly eye on changes. Using a password for the wiki, which can then be placed on the front page, or simply requiring users to create a login to edit content will eliminate most of the spam traffic you might encounter. There is a small but definite learning curve to using a wiki, but most wikis today have a GUI (graphical user interface) that is so similar to a word processing interface that this presents a small challenge for most people, even if wikis are new to them. Wiki syntax can occasionally make integrating other tools into the wiki challenging, but not impossible, for someone who knows a little about HTML and wiki syntax.

Facebook also has an event-planning option that could be used to advertise, register participants, share photos of the unconference, and archive links to outside information. The privacy options allow you to choose who can see your event (only invitees can see details but everyone can see the event announcement, or only invitees can see any information regarding the event). Facebook also allows you to send mass messages to people who have RSVPed. The normal features, like wall-to-wall communication and event sharing, would make word-of-mouth advertising easy for attendees. Facebook is free at this time, though there are always rumors that may change. The obvious and most crippling challenge of using Facebook is that only people who have Facebook accounts can see the event, register for it, and participate in the conversation about it. There are also privacy concerns when using Facebook, but it can be a wonderful way to market your event, even if you do not use it as the central hub of information for your unconference.

A large organization planning an unconference may have access to project management software, like Basecamp (www.basecamp hq.com) or Google Groups (www.groups.google.com), which can facilitate the planning process and possibly other aspects of the unconference as well. Project management software would likely only be accessible within the organization and would require that all participants have accounts and know how to use the software. Project management software can perform a wide variety of tasks including group document editing, job assignments, document and media file sharing, keeping a calendar featuring timelines, and supervising discussion areas. The tools vary in complexity and price; many employ cloud computing and so require little to no IT support, but depending on the tool and the number of users, some project management software will require a subscription fee. Some, like Basecamp, allow for a limited number of projects and users can try the tool for free.

Planning for the Event's Activities

The event phase of the unconference will require a means to foster community and communication, capture the event (audio, visual, online, or all three!), and provide a means for archiving products produced for and during the unconference. If your participants are technologically savvy, you may only need to provide a hub online where they can post and share information. Some groups with knowledge of online tools will make their own decisions, as a group and individually, regarding where, how, and what to share with other unconference participants. Groups with less experience may need some guidance in this area.

Community is not something that begins the first day of the unconference. Community can be fostered weeks before the event by providing a venue for the participants to talk, create, and share.

As an organizer of the event, you can give these conversations a push by asking questions of people as they register, by giving out frequent updates about the event, or by simply encouraging participants to talk to each other. Many unconferences require that registrants list interests or topics for discussion at the time of registration. The list of registrants should be on prime real estate, on a top-level page of the unconference's web presence, which gives the participants importance and makes the list easy to find and browse. Given the focused topic areas of most unconferences and the small number of participants, people who attend may already know or be familiar with each other professionally. It is highly probable that participants will be interested to see what other people have listed as possible topic areas.

Community is fostered more easily at smaller gatherings like an unconference, but it still needs a breeding ground. Include a discussion area in your unconference's web presence for a simple way to provide a marketplace in which to share ideas. This discussion area may also be used during and after the event to continue conversations that are cut short or for participants to ask follow-up questions after the event. Wikis have a built-in discussion area for each page, which can be easily adapted for this purpose. If you are using a multiblogging tool, then you can ask participants to introduce themselves in a post and tell the community why they want to attend the unconference, explain what they hope to get out of the event, or what they hope to give others during the event. Providing a place that is open, fun, and relaxing does not assure you that your community will become talkative, but it is the way to push them in that direction.

A good unconference should also have a lively and active backchannel. By definition a backchannel is like the back door, where people sneak in and then escape in order to have side conversations. Backchannels often happen organically at technology-heavy gatherings, through linked people on Twitter or in large group chat rooms. Hashtags, a tagging system unique to Twitter, will give you a way to aggregate the Twitter backchannel as discussed earlier, but you can also provide an official backchannel for participants to use. It may seem like an oxymoronic move to provide an official venue for an unofficial conversation, but it can work—and may also provide you with a way to archive some of this ongoing conversation. Using a Meebo Room (www.meebo.com) embedded into your unconference wiki or blog is also a great way to provide an official backchannel, and some live blogging tools, like CoveritLive (www.coveritlive.com), also allow for this kind of archiving. You will not be able to control all conversation, and that is not a problem, because an unconference is not about control.

One benefit of having much of your unconference covered live through conversations and archived in various ways is that people who are unable to attend the event will still be able to learn and contribute. People can participate in the conversation even if they are not physically there during the event. After the event, people can continue to talk, ask questions, and learn from the archived material. Unconferences have the potential to build communities. It is amazing how events can continue to make an impact on people months and sometimes years after an event because of something they learned in archived material. This is one reason to consider keeping the information and archived material as open as possible. You should also encourage participants to release content created for and during the event under a Creative Commons license that allows people to share the information when proper attribution is given.

Planning for After the Unconference

The last stage of the unconference is the aftermath, or the archiving phase. If it is of the utmost importance that every scrap of data be saved from the event, be sure to choose tools that self-archive, or that save data indefinitely. A multi-user chat client, for example, may not save an entire history if there are multiple sessions over one or two days. Self-archiving tools include a variety of wikis, blogs, chat clients, live blogging (chat, audio, and video) tools, and photo sharing sites. A warning: If you feel the need to control where every bit of information about your event goes during and after your event, then perhaps you should choose a different kind of event to host. Ultimately, an unconference is about lack of control and letting chaos organize itself in a meaningful way. Often, how the chaos gathers into different places will tell you a lot about the people at your event and the success of the unconference.

There will be official and unofficial products created during the unconference, and you want a way to gather them in one place. Not all unconferences will inspire an avalanche of content. The content and its amount will depend on the kind of event you have and on the people who attend. The information shared and the things produced during the event will be dispersed in many areas of the web, under the ownership of many different people. Instead of trying to control the where and how, simply ask people to tag things in a particular way so that a simple search in a few key places will turn up conversations and items related to your unconference. Participants should be told the common vernacular tagging system for photos, documents, and presentations. Make sure that the tag is usable in many tools, including Flickr, Facebook, WordPress, and Twitter. In Twitter, these tags are called hashtags and are preceded by a # sign. The hashtag for the first American Library Association Unconference was *#unala09*, while the tag for other items was *unala09*. Some tools will gather and display hashtags in real time. CoveritLive, for example, will create a group chat box that incorporates an RSS feed of a particular hashtag, which brings the conversation from two places into one location.

You can do this with RSS feeds or you can request that people add links to the things that they have created to the central hub. There are benefits and drawbacks to both of these methods, and as usual something in the middle will yield the best outcome.

There are a couple of different ways to bring all the content to one central place. Participants, especially those who present, should be asked to link their content to the unconference website. Conversation, photos, and other media can be pulled in on that speaker's page. Many tools have RSS built in, and you can easily pull an RSS feed from a photo site, blogging site, or presentation-sharing site. Adding the RSS feeds to the central site of the unconference may or may not be problematic, as RSS feeds are more easily integrated into some programs than others. Wikis occasionally do not play well with HTML coding, in which RSS is written, and you may find that integrating it into your wiki is frustrating. If you do have problems adding RSS, you can always default back to adding links in a central place and letting your participants choose what information they will follow. Some tools will generate their own RSS feeds; adding feeds to these and then pushing out the new content to participants is made easy. Blogs and some content management software are capable of this. Using RSS is a good choice if you cannot rely on the participants, because of time or technology experience, to add links to the content they have created.

Relying on the group to add content to a central place is a great choice. This allows the participants to use whatever tools they are already familiar with and then they can share their content with the group at their leisure. Employing this method will, of course, result in some content never being gathered due to lack of motion by individual participants. Participant-driven archiving is much less work for organizers, however, and so this is often a much easier way to gather content. The amount of content not gathered to the hub may be negligible as long as the organizers follow the basics for choosing good technology programs. If you are hoping for the participants to do most of the archiving, they should have some say in the choice of program used for the hub. They should also be familiar with the program; it should be comparatively easy to use for the level of the participants and they should retain some control over their content.

In general, people want to share what they have created, especially if it helps others, but you have to make it easy for them to do so and not create unnecessary barriers. People who invest in the site by adding information will also feel more connected to the group. This will help the group to function like a community and possibly allow for growth after the event is long over.

Open access to the archived content is another option that you should consider for your unconference for a few reasons. As discussed many times in this chapter, open content allows people who could not attend your event to use the content to learn and explore the ideas that surfaced there. Unconferences are not only about the actual event. What people do with what is discussed and created days, weeks, or months after the event can be the most important outcome of an unconference. An unconference is subversive, and subversion is always lurking on the edges of changing the world. Changing the world is an admirable goal about which every unconference should dream. The original participants should always have access to the content, but allowing outsiders access will open up new minds and possibilities.

Open access to the unconference's content results in people being able to see the multitude of ideas shared and the fun the participants had. Your event may inspire others to hold similar events or encourage people to attend the next event, should you choose to have one. Open content is free marketing. Lastly, allowing access to the content of the unconference gives the participants something they can point back to and say, "I was there. I did that." This is more important for professions that are required to jump through many hoops to gain longevity, academia being the best example of this.

Because of the wide variety of unconferences and the chaos out of which they grow, it is sometimes easier to imagine them with some firm examples in hand. If this chapter has been too amorphous, too general, and too chaotic for you detail-oriented types, the next chapter, with concrete examples of successful unconferences and camps, is for you.

CHAPTER FIVE

Unconference Case Studies

Have you ever been introduced to a new board or card game and heard the leader say, "It will make more sense once we play."? Unconferences and camps are like that: They make more sense when you actually have seen one in action and witnessed the chaos transforming into something amazing, something great. This really can be a singular experience for everyone involved, and this is the reason that once people go to an unconference or camp, they hunger for that experience again and again.

The following sections provide case studies ranging from Foo Camp, the one that gave the movement legs, to smaller camps, which are held about all topics imaginable in every corner of the world. These are camps and unconferences in action. The unconferences and camps featured employ a wide variety of methods, came into being for many different reasons, and cover many topics and professions. They all have two things in common: a need to share information with others and a belief that everyone has something worthy to contribute.

Foo Camp

If history had to point to the unconference that made chaos hip, it would definitely be Foo Camp (wiki.oreillynet.com/foocamp05/index.cgi). Foo stands for "Friends of O'Reilly," and Foo Camp came into being because Tim O'Reilly and Sara Winge wanted to create a place where interesting people with interesting projects could gather and learn. On the original wiki from the 2003 Foo Camp, O'Reilly says that it started out as a "lark."[1] Foo Camp is an invitation-only gathering of 250 people, and each year the invitation list varies so that there are fresh, new faces mixed in with the veterans. This ensures that there are always new and exciting ideas circulating, and also means that up-and-comers are given a chance to make important connections with established members. In exchange, experienced participants are invigorated by the sparkling new passion of the newbies. Foo Camp has become legendary among geeks. Everyone dreams about getting a coveted invitation to the who's who of techie geekdom.

Fooers camp at the O'Reilly headquarters in Sebastopol, California, for one weekend each year. The invitees are warned, "Foo Camp is as good as participants make it. Be prepared to lead or participate in a session, ask interesting questions, show off what you're working on, and generally leave your mark on the weekend."[2] There are no spectators or quiet "sit-in-the-back-row" people allowed at Foo Camp. This policy ensures that everyone shares, participates, learns, and goes home with a brain bursting with possibilities. People who are lucky enough to get invited to Foo Camp are cutting-edge innovators, so it's not sheer luck that people who attend Foo Camp frequently become big names or that their products become popular. Past Foo Camp attendees include Jimmy Wales, founder of Wikipedia, and Scott Beale, founder of Laughing Squid. The people invited to Foo Camp are passionate about what they do, and they bring their passion with them to *everything* they do. Foo Campers spend a weekend sharing ideas and excitement about new technology.

O'Reilly provides many different kinds of spaces for the event. The camping area is in a large, green, open space: Foo Campers actually camp in tents in the yard of O'Reilly's headquarters. One of the most important items to bring listed on the Foo Camp wiki is a towel. You are expected to come and share your passion for technology, but you still have to maintain personal hygiene! Besides the camping area, there are conference rooms, open areas, and meeting tents outside. Some of the areas have projectors, but participants are encouraged to bring whatever equipment they can to help out. In addition to bringing camping equipment and toiletries, people are asked to provide a laptop, camera, pen and paper, and anything else they need. Participants can also bring things for the "Free Box," a place where you can put swag you no longer want or need, for others to treasure.[3]

O'Reilly provides the space and the food. The participants provide everything else. The spaces used for the camp are flexible: a conference room, larger meeting rooms, outdoor tents, and open spaces. Campers meet in the place that fits their needs for the gathering they are creating. The flexibility in Foo Camp content and space is one aspect that makes it so successful. Campers have the essentials, passion, ideas, technology, and time to make the event something unique.

There are few scheduled events at Foo Camp and most of those are social in nature. Early on the Friday of the event, the schedule board goes up. The schedule board is nothing but a large, blank paper grid. People who want to run a session simply sign up in an allotted time with their topic. Spaces are left open for people who arrive later on Friday.

Figure 5.1 is a picture of the Saturday morning schedule at the 2005 Foo Camp. Notice that some put more information in their square than others, some are funny, some are descriptive, and some are rearranged with new paper and tape. This is chaos and learning at its best, where even the schedule reveals the personalities of the participants.

There are plenty of fun activities that are scheduled, and plenty that are not. Foo Camp is not just about information sharing, it is

Figure 5.1

It is hard to decide what I like best about this photo: the session attached onto a square with duct tape, or the session on the bottom right-hand corner entitled "How F*&%$#% Are We?" This schedule board shows one of the hallmarks of Foo Camp: It does not take itself too seriously. (Photo by Quentin Stafford-Fraser, www.qandr.org/quentin)

also about the connections between the participants. People come to Foo Camp to learn and share, but they also go to meet their peers. In a profession that lives much of its life online, it is powerful to meet in person after building relationships virtually. Some of the other activities at Foo Camp include musical jam sessions, Werewolf (a card game also sometimes called Mafia), board games, beer and scotch tastings, and whiskey shoot-offs. A seasoned Foo Camper suggested getting extra sleep prior to the Camp weekend because the best conversations happen late at night.[4] Most importantly, Foo Campers have fun!

Foo Camp continues to be an important driving force in the technology field because O'Reilly allows the participants to share and learn with no boundaries. Foo Camp is the precursor of what we know as unconferences today, because it was and continues to be so successful. O'Reilly picks great people to be a part of something unique, and in the past few years he has also begun to host themed Foo Camps. Foo Camp is an example of how a self-organizing group of people can share, learn, and change the world—literally.

BarCamp

BarCamp (www.barcamp.org) was created by attendees of some of the first Foo Camps who wanted to expand the idea beyond the 250 people that received a coveted invitation. Because the invite list at Foo Camp changes every year to include newbies, this means that some people do not get to come back. These campers missed Foo Camp so much that they decided to start their own camp trend. BarCamp has become so successful that it has created its own style of unconference.

The first BarCamp was held in Palo Alto, California, in August 2005, and the entire event for 200 people was organized and held in less than one week.[5] BarCamp definitively proves that an event with the potential to change the world does not take months and years to plan. According to the official BarCamp wiki, the name stems from the commonly used coder term "foobar" and is also a nod to Foo Camp.[6] Since 2005, BarCamps have been held all over the world, in virtually every country. BarCamp made the format of Foo Camp accessible to the masses, as a come-as-you-are gathering for anyone interested in technology, coding, open source, and web applications.

BarCamps are usually one-day events with a schedule that is determined by the participants on the day of the event. The schedule is created on a blank grid sheet like the one at Foo Camp. Attendance is usually limited due to the size of the venue, and participants at a BarCamp sign up to attend on a wiki before the event.

Attendance is on a first-come, first-serve basis, and is free; organizers usually find sponsors to cover the cost of the venue and technology needs. When you sign up to attend, you have to include a list of interests and topics on which you are willing to present. Simple and effective introductions at BarCamp are done with three-word tags: You stand up, state your name, and add three tags that describe who you are or what you do. All BarCamps are listed by city and date on the official BarCamp site (www.barcamp.org). The size and length of a BarCamp depends on the organizers and the facility where the event is held. The San Francisco BarCamp, for instance, is held over a weekend, Foo Camp style, with participants camping at one of the Microsoft buildings.[7]

There are few rules at a BarCamp. Like any good unconference, the rules are delivered with humor in the style of *Fight Club*:

- 1st Rule: You do talk about BarCamp.

- 2nd Rule: You do blog about BarCamp.

- 3rd Rule: If you want to present, you must write your topic and name in a presentation slot.

- 4th Rule: Only three-word intros.

- 5th Rule: As many presentations at a time as facilities will allow.

- 6th Rule: No prescheduled presentations, no tourists.

- 7th Rule: Presentations will go on as long as they have to or until they run into another presentation slot.

- 8th Rule: If this is your first time at BarCamp, you *have* to present. (OK, you don't really *have* to, but try to find someone to present with, or at least ask questions and be an interactive participant.)[8]

The rules reveal the nature of BarCamp and the underlying reasons why BarCamp works. It works because people are invested in the process; people are passionate about their interests, and they want to participate. New participants are strongly encouraged to contribute. This is not a "talking heads club"; this is a "talking audience" event. The 4th Rule, which states that only three-word introductions are allowed, reinforces the equal playing field. Each person, no matter how big their ego, is given no more than three words, or tags, with which to define and introduce himself. There are no soliloquy introductions allowed at BarCamp. Participants are encouraged to write, blog, and take pictures during the event, which is the only way that the BarCamp is documented and shared—but you will find pages and pages of documentation with a simple Google search. There are no walls to hop over or fees to pay for access to the information.

One of the stated goals of BarCamp is to share the knowledge learned at BarCamp with the world. This simple vision—that anyone should be welcome in an open community to share ideas and then use those ideas to change the world—is changing the way people view conferences. After helping to organize a BarCamp event in Toronto, Mark Kuznicki coined the phrase "open creative communities" in an effort to understand the ways in which self-organizing groups were coming together to learn and share knowledge.[9] An open creative community is open to anyone, but is held together by participants' interests and creativity. It can be scaled globally or locally and requires only participation and passion. BarCamps, which focus on technology, have been adapted to many different interests. On the official BarCamp wiki, you can find information on camps for many different groups, some far removed from technology. BarCamp is more than an unconference: It is a movement. These adaptations by many different professions, interest groups, and nonprofit organizations are proof that the method of BarCamp—sharing passion to change the world—has even more of an impact than those first BarCampers imagined.

THATCamp and PodCamp

There are many, many derivatives of BarCamp. THATCamp (www.thatcamp.org) and PodCamp (www.podcamp.pbworks.com) stand out because they have spurred their own movements and offshoots. Both of these unconferences have similar styles, guidelines, and scheduling schemes to the original BarCamp.

PodCamp is an unconference event lasting 1 or 2 days. Despite the name, PodCamp covers much more than podcasting; topics can include any social networking technology or new media. For those unfamiliar with these buzzwords, that means topics can include blogs, YouTube, photo sharing, social networks, Twitter, wikis, video blogging, and, of course, podcasting. PodCamps are unique in that they do not cater only to the super-geeky. Newbies to social media are encouraged to attend, and most organizers make an effort to ensure that some of the information presented is on a beginner level. PodCamp is a fabulous way for people to attend a technology boot camp, and there is a PodCamp event held somewhere almost every month. Some PodCamp communities continue long after the event and have evolved into information-sharing entities that just happen to hold an unconference every year. PodCamp Pittsburgh (see Figure 5.2) calls itself an unconference community, maintains a blog with regular entries and regular meetups, and is currently planning its fifth unconference.[10] This group has evolved beyond an annual gathering into a community that supports and educates each other (see Figure 5.3).

THATCamp brings the BarCamp-style unconference to the humanities. The leap from a purely technology-related group to a group interested in how technology affects a discipline and social interactions is fascinating. This leap is important because it shows that the idea of unconferences is not relegated to the geeks and coders alone. THATCamp was started at George Mason University at the Center for History and New Media. Its name stands for the Humanities and Technology Camp. THATCamp attracts a wide

Figure 5.2

PodCamp Pittsburgh has fun and knows not to take itself too seriously, as evidenced by the choice of T-shirt model. (Photo by Rob de la Cretaz, robjdlc.com)

range of participants including "academics, librarians, archivists, cultural activists, curators, students (grad or undergrad), educators, developers, and professionals in all fields where technology and the humanities collide."[11] THATCamps are usually limited regarding the number of participants they can handle. Instead of participating on an open wiki like other BarCamp-style events, THATCampers have to apply for a spot. The application usually includes interest areas and what the participant would like to share with other campers. THATCamp 2010 had 100 participants. By the middle of 2011, THATCamps were being planned in Saigon, Switzerland, Montreal, and in many places around the United States. Regional THATCamps are small, with only 50 to 75 participants. Participants may be chosen by application, but sessions are still planned the day of the event. Like BarCamp, THATCamp is free to attend.

Figure 5.3

Upcoming PodCamps:

- PodCamp Cleveland 2011—Saturday, April 30, 2011
- PodCamp London 2011 - Saturday June 11, 2011
- PodCamp New Hampshire - Saturday and Sunday August 13th and 14th, 2011 at New Hampton School, New Hampton, NH
- PodCamp Montreal - September 2011
- PodCamp Denver 2 - October 7-8, 2011
- PodCamp Cincinnati—October, 2011 near Cincinnati, OH

Past PodCamps:

- PodCamp Nashville - March 26 2011
- PodCamp Toronto 2011 - February 26 & 27, 2011 in Toronto, ON, Canada at Ryerson University
- PodCamp Western MA 3 - Saturday, Feb 5, 2011 on the Westfield St campus in Westfield MA (hash tag #pcwm)
- PodCamp Boulder 3 -- February 4-5, 2011
- Podcamp Halifax 3 -- Sunday January 23, 2011
- PodCamp AZ 2010- November 20 and 21, 2010 @ The University of Advancing Technology, Tempe, AZ
- PodCamp Topeka—November 6, 2010 at Topeka & Shawnee County Public Library in Topeka, KS
- PodCamp NH 2010—October 23 and 24, 2010 at Portsmouth Events Center, Portsmouth, NH.
- PodCamp Connecticut—October 16, 2010 in New Haven at the cool, new Co-op Arts & Humanities Magnet School
- PodCamp Montreal—RESCHEDULED. September 11-12, 2010 at UQAM's Cœur des sciences in Montreal, QC, Canada
- PodCamp Pittsburgh 5—September 18-19, 2010 at the Art Institute of Pittsburgh in Pittsburgh, PA
- PodCamp Boston 5—September 25–26, 2010 at Microsoft NERD in Cambridge, MA
- PodCamp Denver 1—October 1-2, 2010 at Manmade Media Studio in Aurora, CO.
- Podcamp Philly 4- October 1-2, 2010 at Temple University, PA
- PodCamp Ohio 3 - June 19, 2010 at The Ohio State University, Columbus, OH (combined with WordCamp Columbus 2)
- PodCamp London 2 - May 8th, 2010 at The Convergence Center, UWO Research Park, London, Ontario, Canada.
- Podcamp San Antonio 4 - May 8, 2010 (tentative)
- Podcamp Cleveland 2010 (Website) - May 1st, 2010 at Cuyahoga Valley Career Center
- PodCamp Salt Lake City v3 - March 26, 2010 at Neumont University
- PodCamp Fort Collins 1 (Website) (Registration) - March 12 and 13, 2010 at Cohere, LLC
- PodCamp Nashville - March 6, 2010
- PodCamp Toronto 2010 - February 20 & 21, 2010, Toronto, ON, Canada at Ryerson University
- Podcamp Halifax 2 - January 24, 2010 in Dartmouth NS, Canada
- Podcamp Boulder 2 - January 22-23, 2010 in Boulder, CO
- PodCamp Western Mass 2 - February 6, 2010 at Westfield State College, Westfield, MA
- PodCamp AZ 2009 - November 14 & 15th, 2009 @ The University of Advancing Technology, Tempe, AZ
- PodCamp NH - November 7th & 8th, 2009
- PodCamp Pittsburgh 4 - October 10 & 11, 2009 at Art Institute of Pittsburgh (Directions to AIP)
- Podcamp Philly 3- October 3 & 4th, 2009 at Temple University
- PodCamp Montreal - September 19-20, 2009 in Montreal, QC, Canada

In these listings, notice the frequency with which PodCamps are held and the cities represented. (Screenshot taken from www.podcamp.pbworks.com by author)

GovCamp Canada 2010

Though technology does often facilitate the planning and distribution of information, the camp format is increasingly being used by ordinary citizens to change their communities. In Canada, groups are currently meeting under the banner of GovCamp Canada (www.govcamp.ca), which is part of the larger open government movement. The open government movement calls for transparency in government workings and increased participation from individual citizens. This idea has taken on a newfound urgency in an age where information is so readily available at the fingertips of ordinary citizens. GovCamp Canada is a type of ChangeCamp unconference, an open community movement in Canada (www.changecamp.ca). The purpose of ChangeCamp is to foster nonpartisan government participation by individual "citizens, policy-makers, technologists, design-thinkers, change agents and media creators."[12] At one of the first ChangeCamps, held in January 2009, community activists and local government officials met and discussed what information the city should be offering online, among other topics. The officials wanted to know what the technologists in the groups could create from such information. These types of conversations have encouraged the local governments in Canada to offer more information, like vehicle tracking and traffic updates, available in open formats to programmers.[13] ChangeCamp is focused on community change and government, while GovCamp Canada focuses on promoting openness in local and national government.

In 2010, there were two GovCamps held in Canada, one in Ottawa on May 31 and June 1, and one in Toronto on June 17. GovCamp Ottawa involved a combination of keynotes, panel discussions, interviews, live questions from an online audience, and breakout sessions. Topics for the breakout sessions were proposed the day of the camp by participants. Some of the topics included

- Measuring the impact of open gov data. Are there examples, success stories?

- Deciding where we are going with open gov. How important is leadership from the top?

- Implementing technology and pondering policy. Do we achieve our goals with tech or planning?[14]

A video of the panel discussion with questions is available on the GovCamp Ottawa event page (govcamp.ca/ottawa-govcamp-post-event), along with a grid of the breakout sessions and a link to a transcript of the ongoing conversation under the hashtag *#govcamp*.

The Ottawa event held a live question-and-answer session from an online-only audience. Questions came from people who submitted them via the Twitter hashtag *#govcamp*, and then the responses were transmitted via live video feed. The questions, some of which you can see on the GovCamp Ottawa event page, are thoughtful and provoking, and show that people are very interested in making their government function better without delving into the mire of politics itself. This particular use of Twitter and live video is interesting because the target audience was not people at the physical meeting, but interested citizens online. By including this type of event, GovCamp was able to expand the group of people able to participate in the conversation. Anyone with a computer and a Twitter account was able to add to this vibrant community that came together for a day to make its government better.

The GovCamp Toronto meeting was different from its Ottawa counterpart. It took place over the course of 4 hours in the evening, and there were brief opening and closing remarks, small group discussions, and web and mobile application demonstrations. In addition to citizens, technologists, and activists, participants included the chief information officers for the cities of Edmonton and Toronto and the director of marketing and communications from the Cabinet Office of Ontario. This was not a meeting of fringe activists, but a serious meeting of people from all levels of the citizenry and government who believe in the ability of openness to create a better government.

In June 2011, GovCamp Canada (govcamp.eventbrite.com) hosted another event focused on creating community between the citizens and the government. This event included an Open Data Apps Showcase for developers. GovCamp Canada, with its support at multiple levels, has the potential to change the conversation about government in Canada.

Social Software Showcase

Some ideas are born out of rebellion and a wish for something better than what is currently offered. As with most other large conferences, in order to present a topic at the American Library Association (ALA), you have to be invited or sponsored by a committee, interest group, or division, and need to present your proposal a year in advance through an official planning committee. This system ensures that any technology topic presented will never be emerging or new, and is rarely exciting.

In 2007, I was one of three leaders of a group called BIGWIG, an interest group focused on new media and social software in libraries. BIGWIG stands for the Blogs, Interactive Groupware Wikis Interest Group, but since technology is always changing, it has evolved into the social software and new media interest group of the ALA's Library and Information Technology Association, or ALA LITA. Librarians love acronyms as much as engineers, so the full title of this group is ALA LITA BIGWIG! We decided it was time to subvert an outdated system and wanted a way to present cutting-edge technology topics to an engaged audience. In three months, we planned the first BIGWIG Social Software Showcase (showcase.litablog.org). We asked some of the smartest librarians we knew to come up with some sort of online presentation about the technology topic or tool about which they were the most excited. These presentations were put up on a wiki during the week of ALA's annual conference. We blogged, we tweeted (which was still really new in 2007), and we chatted up our non-presentation presentations.

There was no podium at the Social Software Showcase, just a room full of round tables with the topics printed on tent cards. The presenters gave an elevator pitch of their topic and then sat down at different tables, and participants were then free to walk around the room and join any of the discussions going on during the event. There was no advertising for the event except for word of mouth online. The Social Software Showcase as an event was not in the official ALA Annual 2007 program, but still attracted 50 people to talk about emerging technology and libraries. There was a backchannel during the event, and we did have some people chatting with us from afar. Only a few days after the physical event, the wiki had logged more than 7,000 hits. This was amazing for an event with no advertising except the chatter occurring online. For us, we counted it as a win because we had people in a room, engaged in passionate conversations about new and emerging technologies.

The Social Software Showcase has evolved since that first experimental year. The Showcase was so popular and received so much great buzz that it got some support from the official planning committees, is now in the printed and online program for ALA Annual, and has become a regular event that is part of the larger overall conference. Instead of BIGWIG leaders choosing the topics and presenters, the topics are now chosen by anyone who wants to participate. Members of ALA, BIGWIG, or even lurkers, can suggest and vote on topics to be discussed at upcoming showcases. This discussion and voting happens about 2 months prior to the conference. After the topics are chosen, BIGWIG finds people doing interesting things in that topic area or with that technology. Often people volunteer to speak as topics are suggested or once they see the winning list of technologies.

We have tried different formats with various degrees of success. The first year, participants freely joined ongoing discussion groups at round tables in one large room. This was relaxed, but resulted in the presenters having to go over similar points in the discussion over and over as new people came and went. The second year, the presenters were at stations and the audience rotated every 10 minutes or so. That meant that the speakers had to give their presentations and answer questions in a short amount of time, which actually worked quite well. This event was never, ever meant to be about talking heads. In fact, one of our favorite pictures from that first year was of the empty podium (see Figure 5.4). The drawback of the audience moving around was that it took a lot longer for the attendees, whose numbers had swelled considerably after the first year, to move and get settled. In 2009, the audience was split into equal parts and the presenters traveled to different groups around the room to give their talks. This format seemed to result in much less chaos for the attendees.

Simultaneous to the physical event, BIGWIG adds online elements to the Social Software Showcase. There are backchannels, online videos, discussion boards, Twitter hashtags, and many other ways to participate in the discussion regardless of whether you can

Figure 5.4

No talking heads means no falling asleep and wondering where the closest coffee can be found. (Photo by author)

attend the physical event. Often, the online discussion rivals the in-person conversations in intensity and creativity.

The Social Software Showcase is still planned by a small handful of people in less than 3 months and has evolved into an event that is more like Speed Geeking. The modern version of that original gathering is organized at the BIGWIG website (www.yourbigwig.com/showcase). The topics are proposed and chosen before the event by the participants, who use an online forum to vote. During the showcase, presenters move around the room to groups of 50 to 100 people, giving short presentations and then doing a Q&A period. Its success has convinced the ALA that this format is an important addition to the regular conference fare. It could be argued that the next case study in this chapter, the ALA Unconference, is the direct result of BIGWIG deciding that chaos and immediacy were better than talking heads and dusty information.

ALA Unconference

In 2009, the ALA hosted its first unconference (www.wikis.ala.org/annual2009/index.php/Unconference) associated with its large annual conference in Chicago, Illinois. This unconference stands out from previous examples because, though the schedule was chosen by the group, it was determined before the physical event. Registration was open to any ALA member and limited to 75 participants. The event was announced a few weeks prior to registration on various official and unofficial communications. Registration was handled like BarCamp, on a first-come, first-serve basis on the main conference's wiki. Once registration was full, there was a waiting list, and participants had to sign up to volunteer to either present on a topic or facilitate a roundtable discussion on a topic.

An unconference was a new concept to many of the participants and to the sponsoring organization, so the organizers, Meredith Farkas and I, wanted the day to have some predetermined structure. We created a schedule with blank time slots. There were 10 lightning talks, at 7 minutes each with 5 minutes for questions. These slots were given in two chunks, one in the morning and one in the afternoon. There were also three different discussion periods, lasting 50 minutes each, during which there were 10 roundtable discussions. Topics for both the presentations and discussions were determined by the participants' votes. We used SurveyMonkey (www.survey monkey.com) as a data tool, and participants were asked to vote for their top three choices of presentation and discussion topics.

Most of the communication to participants before the event was done via the wiki. The survey of the topics was emailed directly. Participants were encouraged to create profiles on the wiki, and presenters and discussion facilitators were encouraged to link their presentation or information to the wiki for others, especially for those who could not attend the physical event. During the unconference, we used CoveritLive (www.coveritlive.com) as a multichat tool and encouraged the use of the tag and hashtag *#unala09* on Twitter, Flickr, and other social media sites. CoveritLive was able to integrate tweets from Twitter if they were marked with the official hashtag. For the presentations, we had a traditional projector and podium.

ALA Unconference 2009 was successful, though it did not run as smoothly in some areas as it did in others. The event was kept on schedule during the Lightning Talks, which ensured that every presenter received equal time. Lightning Talks are really a wonderful thing. If one presentation does not interest you, another one will be along in a few short minutes. Unfortunately, the wireless for the event was limited to the number of people who could be logged in, and this was an issue for everyone. Wireless was essential for the backchannel and live blogging and so these two elements also suffered. The lunch break was two hours, because we provided lunch and we wanted people to be able to chat and mingle. In hindsight, this was too long and we lost some people to the long break. The Law of Two Feet worked against us in this way.

It was successful enough, however, that ALA has held two subsequent unconferences in conjunction with larger conferences and has plans for more in the future.[15]

Mashup Camp

Mashup Camp, "the unconference for the uncomputer," is an unconference that takes place over three days with three separate themes: Learn, Hack, and Compete (www.mashupcamp.com). Mashup Camp is definitely a coding-heavy, geek camp for mashup developers and technology gurus. They define the uncomputer this way: "The internet now encapsulates the most interesting, intriguing and ultimately useful (in terms of the stuff that people need in their applications) APIs, as compared to the computers and their collection of programmable APIs. The source of an API (or the variety of APIs used by a mashup) can be the server on your local area network or a machine halfway across the world. We call it the 'uncomputer.'"[16] API (which stands for application programming interface) is, at its most basic definition, the way in which information is shared between two different programs to create a new program or display of information.

Mashup Camp originated from a conversation between David Berlind, currently a writer at *Information Week*, and Eleanor Kruszewski, of the Yahoo! Developer Network, at an after-hours party during IDG World Expo on December 12, 2005. They wanted to create a free conference around APIs for developers. With the help of their friend Doug Gold, they launched the first Mashup Camp in February 2006.[17]

The format of Mashup Camp is unique in that it is a mixture of predetermined presentations, participant-driven sessions, and a mashup contest, with the winner determined by the participants via vote by wooden nickel. The first day, titled Learn, is filled with presentations by juggernauts in the uncomputer movement. Participants attend sessions and learn about the newest developments in

mashups. The second day, Hack, starts with the participants deciding the course of the rest of the day. There are five discussion periods during which nine discussions run simultaneously. Discussion
periods are decided on, BarCamp style, with discussion leaders
adding their topic to a grid.[18] The last day, Compete, involves a
show-and-tell session where hackers can show off their latest
mashup. Campers vote on the mashup of their choice by giving a
wooden nickel to their favorite group.

Endnotes

1. Tim O'Reilly, "Why Foo," O'Reilly Media, wiki.oreillynet.com/foocamp05/
   index.cgi?WhyFoo (accessed July 19, 2011).

2. "Welcome to Foo Camp," O'Reilly Media, wiki.oreillynet.com/foocamp08/
   index.cgi?HomePage (accessed July 19, 2011).

3. "What to Bring," O'Reilly Media, wiki.oreillynet.com/foocamp08/index.cgi?
   WhatToBring (accessed July 19, 2011).

4. "Tips From Seasoned Campers," O'Reilly Media, wiki.oreillynet.com/foo
   camp07/index.cgi?TipsFromSeasonedFooCampers (accessed July 19, 2011).

5. "Bar Camp," Wikipedia, en.wikipedia.org/wiki/BarCamp (accessed July 19,
   2011).

6. "About Us," BarCamp, www.barcamp.org/About-Us (accessed July 19, 2011).

7. "BarCamp San Francisco," BarCamp, www.barcamp.org/BarCampSan
   Francisco (accessed July 19, 2011).

8. Tanek Celik, "The Rules of BarCamp," BarCamp, www.barcamp.org/The
   RulesOfBarCamp (accessed July 19, 2011).

9. Mark Kuznicki, "Essay: What Is an Open Creative Community?" Remarkk
   Consulting, remarkk.com/2007/02/25/essay-what-is-an-open-creative-community
   (accessed July 19, 2011).

10. PodCamp Pittsburgh, podcamppittsburgh.com (accessed July 19, 20110).

11. "Contact Details?" THATCamp Southern California, thatcampsocal.org
    (accessed July 19, 2011).

12. "About," ChangeCamp, changecamp.ca/about (accessed July 19, 2011).

13. Ivor Tossell, "Open-Source Politics Breathe Fresh Air Into the Big Smoke,"
    The Globe and Mail, www.theglobeandmail.com/news/technology/article
    969003. ece (accessed July 19, 2011).

14. "The Grid," GovCamp Ottawa, govcamp.ca/site/wp-content/uploads/2010/06/The-Grid.png (accessed July 19, 2011).

15. "Unconference," American Library Association Annual 2010 Conference Wiki, annual.ala.org/2010/index.php?title=Unconference (accessed July 19, 2011).

16 "What Is the Uncomputer?" Mashup Camp Silicon Valley, www.mashupcamp.com/about/#what_is_the_uncomputer (accessed July 19, 2011).

17. "How Did Mashup Camp Originate?" Mashup Camp Silicon Valley, www.mashupcamp.com/about/#how_did_originate (accessed July 19, 2011).

18. "MashupCamp 08 Discussion Grid," Mashup Camp, www.mashupcamp.com/wiki/index.php/MashupCamp8DiscussionGrid (accessed July 19, 2011).

CHAPTER SIX

Applying the Unconference Structure Beyond Conferences and the Future of the Movement

Unconference. Camp. Open creative community. Open Space Technology (OST). The term is not as important as the belief behind the action. This belief, this movement toward action, is more than a simple gathering together of people. It is a belief that the knowledge of the group is equal to or greater than that of the talking head behind the podium, and that people know best how they interact, learn, and apply knowledge that will help them be successful or make their community better.

Foo Camp and BarCamp may have made this method of sharing knowledge popular among geeks, but the ideas are continuing to spread to other fields. The camp idea has even been applied to the missional church.[1] Unconferences will continue to grow in popularity and scope because they give people something they need, something vital that all people desire: the ability to share a passion, have their voices heard, and connect with others. Since people began communicating with words, weaving stories, and creating art, the goal has been to share what we know and what we feel. When a group is able to organize itself and freely share its collective knowledge, amazing things can happen. An unconference gathering can be used to create and communicate different kinds of knowledge and accomplish many different goals.

Unconferences Can Change the Traditional Conference

Unconferences have the ability to bring fresh ideas to a tired conference circuit. For many professionals who attend conferences, the talking head system becomes dull and uninspiring. There is no free flow of ideas when the audience is only a receptacle. Conferences have the potential to be the place where people can go to be refreshed and energized by their profession, not be beaten down with information. If traditional conferences incorporated some unconference elements into their programming, they could add a level of energy not found with a simple speaker behind the podium. People who are able to share their passions with peers and dream out loud are people who will continue to contribute in substantial ways to their profession. Traditional conferences can be uninspiring, and we need our professionals to discover again why they love their jobs. It is hard to continue to be unhappy with your profession when you are actively working with other individuals to make it better, and unconferences offer a much needed place for discussion that traditional conferences lack. Involved people contribute and make a difference in their community, however you define community. The mob knows the needs of their community intimately, they are the ones who want and need to improve, and they are the people who will be passionate about sharing what they know.

Alternate Uses for the Unconference Model

For professional organizations facing a dispirited membership, an unconference could serve as a much-needed energy boost. First, organizations can use the unconference system of self-organization in their strategic planning process. If your membership is unhappy with its current direction, put a large group of members in a room and ask them to find a new path. Holding a camp could yield amazing results for an organization in need of some new ideas, innovations, or just people with passion. People who have chosen their profession out of love may become jaded, but they are still invested in the direction of their field; an unconference could be a way to rejuvenate the jaded and give hope to those who have just joined your organization. An organization that cares about its members is an organization that gives opportunities for the members to share and then listens intently while they do so. Excellent organizations will then take that knowledge, share it widely, and make the changes needed. Self-organization and mob learning are not restricted to conferences.

Many organizations also struggle with strategic planning. Management wants to retain a level of control over the process because they have ideas about where they would like the group to go. Members in the organization want to be able to have input in the process and the outcome because whatever is decided, they are the ones who make it a reality. These two methodologies—control and sharing—are often at odds. Management that listens to membership is a management that has invested in the belief that it will take the ideas of the members to heart. It can be especially disheartening for members to believe they were listened to and then see that nothing different was done. Using the facilitation styles of an unconference in strategic planning can open up doors for everyone in an organization and may produce ideas and directions for the group that would have never have been shared otherwise.

Allowing members to self-organize and place values on the ideas generated in strategic planning sessions means that members, not management, are assigning value to the future of the organization. Every organization wants its members to be passionate about what they do, but members will lose the glow of first love quickly if they realize that their knowledge and opinions are not valued by their organization. Members involved in the process are members that will feel emotionally invested in your organization. This does require that management be willing to give up control over the process. This relinquishment of control to members is likely the reason that more organizations do not employ self-organization. People in management are there to wield some level of power and control, and it is hard to give those things over to chaos.

Management that is hesitant to try something as radical as self-organized strategic planning can incorporate OST facilitation styles into parts of a traditional strategic planning process. Using a Dotmocracy system to explore challenges and ideas in a strategic planning process could be very exciting. Members of an organization can be given opportunities to gather, share, dream, and develop their own directions for the organization. These sessions can be done with little or no facilitation. Management can then take the ideas from these sessions and use them to guide the strategic-planning process. When a process is open and the chance for input great, members are more likely to support the outcome, even if it looks slightly different than their original imaginings. People simply want to know that they are listened to and trusted. Administrations that remember this are much more likely to have members who are willing to share their passion with the rest of the organization.

A large organization going through strategic planning may want to hold sessions using different facilitation styles at different points in the process or with different groups. Large organizations can hold a large, organization-wide gathering followed by many smaller sessions. A large group could be asked to create its own agenda for topic discussion, its own template for dreaming about what does and does not work in its organization. If the organization has challenges to solve, a session about facing these challenges could be held separately from the session in which members are asked to dream and imagine the future of their organization. Sessions in which members are asked to define, confront, and solve challenges facing the organization should be done with careful facilitation so that they do not devolve into a finger-pointing, griping free-for-all. These open meetings should be held to discuss challenges in order to find solutions. A challenging session should never be completed without some ideas that will lead to actions taken to improve the problems. Management of an organization should attend sessions in which challenges are discussed only if they can participate as silent, casual observers. These sessions are about the workers or members and how they feel about problems facing the organization, not about the management fixing the problems or defending the current path and processes.

Smaller sessions held at different levels of the organization give members the opportunity to share with peers how the organization is doing and where it should go in the future. Working groups or already standing committees are a good way to organize these smaller sessions. Smaller groups, with a large degree of established intimacy and power structures, will have some trouble self-organizing. They can, however, be asked to set their own agendas and facilitate their own discussions. Again, if managers, committee chairs, or people in positions of power are present for these smaller gatherings, it is important that they allow the members to lead the discussion.

Using the methodology of OST in a strategic-planning process requires openness and trust. Some organizations may have trust as one of their challenges. Placing faith in your members to design and carry out the process is a great way to begin to heal this issue. Strategic planning should be seen as an opportunity to grow in new ways, not as a process without meaning. If done well, the process of strategic planning can be as influential as the plan itself. Members who have helped define the direction of the organization will be passionate about where they are going, and that passion will impact the organization on all levels.

Staff training is an ongoing, never-ending need in any organization, but it often lacks variety. In most organizations, staff training is done during staff development days, on the job, or one-on-one with a manager. Staff development days are interesting in that the sessions are usually arranged by management, on topics they think their workers need to know, and given by some outside talking head. I have been the talking head in this situation, and although I feel it is a valid way to learn, there are always some resentful people in the audience. The resentfulness usually stems from the workers who think that this is not information they need, or the belief that management is asking them to learn and carry out yet another function in an already busy day.

Some of this resentment can be avoided by simply asking workers what they think they need to know to do their job better. People complain less when you ask them what they want and actually listen to what they say. A worker who is unhappy with training options should be allowed to suggest other options for their professional enhancement. Workers who choose not to participate by giving ideas and opinions have therefore chosen to accept what the rest of the group decides without complaint. Challenges, as discussed earlier in relation to strategic planning, should always be brought forward with solutions. To point out problems without hope or solutions is simply griping and whining, and is counterproductive to any organization. If you are seeking to employ some unconference techniques with your employees or you want your employer to use them, beware of letting gripes and whines take over the process.

▶ ▶ ▶ ▶ *Have a Camp Day Instead of Staff Training*

Name and Details of the Organization: Princeton Public Library (PPL) in Princeton, NJ. 54 FTE serving a population of 31,000.

Problem: The budget for staff training had been drastically cut, but the staff still needed instruction.

Solution: Create a staff-organized training day that would promote team building and be fun.

What They Did: The schedule for the Camp PPL day, held in November 2009, included Lightning Talks by volunteer staff members, 10 Birds of a Feather sessions (facilitated by volunteers) with topics ranging from customer service to healthy habits, and a staff recognition assembly. Many fun activities were planned to promote team building, including a dessert competition with prizes donated by local businesses. During lunch, staff members had the option of joining a Wii tournament, going for a walk outside, or lounging inside. One of the main features of the day, and one of the largest successes, was one of the lowest tech elements. A "PPL Wall" was set up on the wall of the main meeting area. It included different areas for posting thoughts about the topics, and a "map app" where people could indicate places where they had traveled. The most popular part of the Wall was the "Facebook." Staff members had their own profile sections, which included pictures. Throughout the day, people put up notes to and about each other on the Wall, offering encouragement and praise. This also helped staff members who rarely interacted get to know each other better.

How They Did It: A small planning group held brief meetings over the summer prior to the camp. During these staff meetings, the concept of camps/unconferences was introduced. Surveys were sent out to staff asking for topic ideas for sessions and for event volunteers. The topics generated from this survey became another survey, where staff members were asked to vote for their top five topics, and the 10 most popular topics became the Birds of a Feather discussions. To give staff exposure to new technology tools, two different websites were used to create the planning surveys,

Google Forms (part of Google Docs, docs.google.com) and Zoomerang (www.zoomerang.com).

Concrete Results: During one of the Birds of a Feather discussions, it was revealed that the monthly staff meetings were not meeting the needs of the staff. As the hub of their community, PPL hosts many public events each day. It was hard for staff to adequately learn about all of these new events in a timely manner when their main interaction with different departments occurred only once per month. As a result of the Camp PPL discussion, these monthly meetings were canceled and replaced by a daily meeting in the public service area at 9:15. Meetings range from 3 to 10 minutes in length and include a briefing on what is going on in the building that day. Staff members stand for the entire meeting, which encourages brief interactions. If a topic comes up that needs more attention or a conversation in a staff-only area, a longer meeting is scheduled for later in the day or week. Responsibility for these meetings rotate weekly between departments. This new meeting structure has continued for almost a year and is popular with the staff.

Staff Reactions: A follow-up survey was sent out, and feedback was positive. The staff would like to repeat the camp format in a future staff training day.

This information was gathered via email and from an interview from Janie Hermann, public programming coordinator at PPL. See her presentation on Slideshare at www.slideshare.net/JanieH/creating-a-camp-experience-for-staff-development-day.

A self-organized training day could reveal a lot about your employees. If you planned a staff training day, gathered your employees in a room, and told them they were in charge of their own learning experience, what would happen? In many organizations, it is likely that the knowledge gaps of one person can be filled by someone else in the room. Even if the gathering included people from many levels of the organization, there may be similar needs across the board. If you do experiment with this type of learning day, make sure that the people involved have access to different tools, like computers, paper, markers, pens, flip charts, a projector, and snacks. Food is important. In a staff training unconference that includes people from many levels of the organization, people may need to be encouraged to interact with those outside of their normal working groups, and bonding at the snack table is a good way to make connections.

Encourage your employees to continue what they learn during the training unconference. People can organize smaller group meetings after the training, like accountability groups, to which they can report new things they have learned or how they have applied their new knowledge. A lunch group or frequent, informal gatherings can serve this purpose. These gatherings, which may resemble meetings, should be self-organized and not imposed from above. Employees should be given the responsibility for maintaining these groups; they should not be mandated. You want people to feel ownership of their learning experience, not feel as if they have been dragged into it kicking and screaming.

Asking the mob to brainstorm about training will look different for different groups. Send them a survey they can take quickly at their desks. Have a brainstorming session during a meeting. Ask them to anonymously drop cards into a suggestion box. The method you choose will reflect the employees you have and the way they best like to express themselves. There are two things you should keep in mind during the inquiry process. First, always leave a way for people to respond without their peers knowing who it was that suggested the topic. Some employees may not be comfortable flaunting their weaknesses in front of other people. If one person has a knowledge gap in a particular area, they're likely to think they are the only one, even if others have the same problem. Be sensitive to, but not overprotective of, these employees. The second thing to keep in mind is that you want to encourage people to come up with solutions to the lack of knowledge they have in certain areas, so when someone suggests a topic, ask them how they would like to learn about it. If you are doing this in a group setting, face-to-face, or online in some way, encourage other people in the group to suggest solutions as well. For instance, if many of your employees are not comfortable with social software and it is relevant to their job, ask them how they would like to be taught to use it. Would they like to all look at a different aspect of the tool and then share their findings with each other? Is there someone within the organization who could teach this to your group?

People want to be a part of a community. Communities are created within groups that gather for an unconference, and the community often lasts beyond the event or the day because of the way people share and interact at an unconference. The community aspect is important. People want to be a part of something that has meaning. It is a drive that humans have and one that we seek to fill in many ways. Conferences, companies, and organizations that take this need for community and harness it will find that the mob will take them places far and above what they imagined possible.

Whatever you call the movement, the self-organized group is here to change the way we learn and interact with each other. The momentum behind unconferences shows no signs of slowing. As the ideas are shared with other professions and groups, like Toronto's TransitCamp, the methodology of the unconference is applied in unexpected ways.[2] TransitCamp was a gathering of regular citizens who came together to discuss their local transit system, how to improve it, and brainstorm ways to generate interest about mass transit among the citizenry. Toronto TransitCamp was a camp-style meeting hosted by the Toronto Transit Commission; the company received community feedback on some proposed website changes and agreed to release transit information to programmers. Due to TransitCamp, a small community of citizens formed who then continued to meet and discuss ways to make their transit system better.[3]

These are simple, ordinary citizens doing extraordinary things. Because the unconference gathering is so adaptable, there are no limits to its application. Any group of people with a problem to solve or a place to share knowledge and learning can find a style of unconference that reflects both their needs and their personalities. The self-organizing method works outside of the conference circuit as well. Open creative communities such as TransitCamp have the potential to positively affect any challenge we face as a society, from pollution to politics. The mob, with their collective knowledge, has the ability to solve any problem placed before them. The beliefs behind unconferences, that the wisdom of crowds is valuable, that everyone has something important to share, and that a mob can organize themselves into whatever iteration is best for solving the current problem, are beliefs that can be applied anywhere from a board room to the classroom.

In the second half of this book, I explore the learning environment in higher education and within organizations. Staff training and continuing education, in its many forms, and how the power of the mob is changing the way we learn, are discussed in detail.

Endnotes

1. "Welcome to ChurchCamp," ChurchCamp, churchcamp.pbworks.com (accessed July 19, 2011).

2. "Metronauts1," Transit Camp, metronauts.ca (accessed July 19, 2011).

3. Mark Kuznicki, "Enterprise 2.0 Case Study: Toronto Transit Camp," Slideshare, www.slideshare.net/remarkk/enterprise20-case-study-toronto-transit-camp (accessed July 19, 2011).

PART TWO

Changing the Rules of Learning

Throughout the first part of this book, we spent time looking at the ways that participation in the conference process can be enhanced when individuals are given the power and freedom to choose their own paths. In this second half, we examine how the ideas of mob rule can be applied to traditional learning situations in higher education and other places where adults are sent to the classroom.

Over the course of our lives, we spend years in and out of classrooms of various size, quality, and structure. As children, we become students because we are required to do so. As young adults, we often choose to seek a secondary education, attending a college or university. Before entering the workforce, we may naively think that leaving college will mark the end of our classroom days. But once we find a job, we learn that we are again required to attend many more hours of classroom instruction and staff training of one kind or another for the duration of our careers. (Some brave souls even go back to school to earn graduate degrees!) Classrooms, even for adults, are inescapable. And though many adults like learning, many dislike the learning experience.

We spend a large portion of our lives in classrooms, but the methods by which we are taught have not changed much. One of the oldest universities still in existence today, Al-Azhar University in Cairo, Egypt, was founded in 972 AD.[1] Since then, teachers have been standing in front of a group of students and talking. We call this activity lecturing, and perhaps it is no coincidence that *lecture*, which we often use when teaching adults, also has a second definition that means to scold or admonish. A lecture requires no interaction, only passive listening. We all know how hard it is to retain information from a class that consists mainly of listening.

The word *classroom* brings to mind an image of a room with a teacher in the front and students in rows facing front. The teacher is standing and the students are sitting. But, if we redefine what it means to learn, what it means to teach, and what it means to be creative in a learning environment, what could the word *classroom* come to mean in the future? What if you could go to a classroom that was more than the physical space you occupied? Where would you go, and what could you create?

What if you could interact in productive ways with your classmates while the instructor was talking? What if students were allowed to learn from each other in dynamic ways, and in real time? What if we allowed students to create the content of their learning environment? What if the mob was given a topic and allowed to teach themselves? What can the mob bring to the table?

What if the teacher were a guide and shepherd, instead of the locomotive on the train? What if the mob was given the freedom to decide what they needed to learn to make them better employees?

What if we changed everything?

The mob has the capacity, knowledge, and ability to become a self-educating entity that can creatively construct its own learning ecosystem. If we accept that we, the mob, collectively know more than any one individual, we should be able to apply that knowledge toward educating ourselves and our peers. The mob can create and explore, learn and grow, teach and redefine community. It can do all these things, and it can do them in and out of the classroom.

Endnote

1. "Al-Azhar University, Cairo," Islam for Today, www.islamfortoday.com/alazhar.htm (accessed July 19, 2011).

CHAPTER SEVEN

Traditional Classrooms:
What Is Missing?

Traditionally, formal learning has taken place in a classroom with rows of students facing a teacher who is lecturing in a discipline in which he or she is an expert. We have been teaching this way for hundreds of years. Through our primary and secondary education years, into college, and then when we seek to enhance our careers, we primarily have been in classrooms where we have been asked to learn through lecture and listening. Primary and secondary education has changed dramatically in the past couple decades, though, as these fields have sought to include other learning types. The learning environment in the working world, though, is still mostly stagnant. This book will only address university-level learning environments and other classes or workshops populated by professionals seeking to enhance their career. For people attending college classes or other continuing education venues, the lecture-style class is still the norm. Unfortunately, few people learn well in this kind of passive learning environment.

Learning Styles

Understanding adult education and training requires an exploration of learning styles. Learning styles have been defined in many different ways, and definitions have evolved over the years as psychology and education became more complex in their understandings. Learning styles also tend to shift often around generational lines, though I think this has more to do with our understanding of learning and how people are taught in school as children. Once the complexity of learning styles is addressed, it is easy to see how a straight lecture is the wrong way to teach most students.

The simplest way to differentiate learning styles is by separating them into three categories: auditory, visual, or active learning. Auditory learners, a small group, do learn well in a lecture environment. Visual learners need to see something done or see pictures of something to fully understand it. Active learners must complete the task or be involved in some related activity to understand the information. Realistically, most people learn better with a combination of methods. Knowledge acquisition occurs on a deeper level when the learning is student-oriented, as opposed to being centered on the knowledge of the instructor, and when the information is learned through problem solving.[1] The traditional lecture-style class is far away from presenting knowledge in an atmosphere of problem solving.

Learning theories, however, are not always as simple as auditory, visual, or active, and can be much more detailed. In 1984, David Kolb published his well-known Kolb learning styles, which have been widely used since their debut.[2] Kolb adapted and created his styles by using many accepted theories and definitions about creativity and intelligence. According to Kolb, there are two steps in the learning process: taking in an experience and then dealing with that experience. How we choose to absorb new information and then process that information creates the full picture of an individual's learning style. The two different ways to approach an experience are:

- Concrete Experience: Learning by Experiencing

  - Learning from specific events

  - Relating to others

  - Being sensitive to feelings and people

- Abstract Conceptualization: Learning by Thinking

  - Analyzing ideas logically

  - Planning systematically

  - Acting on an intellectual understanding of a situation

The two different ways to deal with the new information following an experience are:

- Reflective Observation: Learning by Reflecting

  - Observing carefully before making judgments

  - Viewing issues from different perspectives

  - Looking for the meaning of things

- Active Experimentation: Learning by Doing

  - Showing ability to get things done

  - Taking risks

  - Influencing people and events through action[3]

In Kolb's explanation of the learning experience, the pull between learning styles is always between the people who want to observe and reflect and the people who want to experience and do. Everyone uses a combination of these learning styles, but there is usually one aspect of learning that appeals to us. Most people are easily able to self-identify their own learning styles, but there are tests that you can take to be certain of the type of learning that suits you best.

A traditional classroom contains a combination of many different learning styles, but we continue to employ the talking head model of education. This may address those who prefer learning through thinking and reflection, but sometimes even reflection is noticeably absent from this methodology. In a true lecture class, the student is simply an input for the knowledge. There is no output phase. A reflective learner will need time and an opportunity to reflect. An active experimenter will need time to create something with the knowledge or to try the new information in the real world. The products created by the students, as they make sense of the new knowledge and their understanding of it, also need a home—some class hub where they can share. We have a greater understanding of personalities and learning styles today, but we do not always approach teaching with this understanding in hand. This failing should not be laid completely at the feet of instructors, because we still fail in many ways to equip our teachers and trainers with the knowledge they need to reach people on many different levels, and we fail to provide them the proper tools to do so.

Few people are passive learners, meaning that most people require some involvement in their learning process. Students need to be able to do something, experiment, or create with newly acquired information. A good teacher will always ask students to "compare, apply, evaluate, analyze, and synthesize, but never to only listen and remember."[4] It is not enough that we ask people to absorb the information we give them; it is in the application of knowledge that the lecture-style class fails. A true teacher requires students to take the information and do something with it, which is the difference between remembering and applying. Do we learn because it may be on the test, or do we learn because we were asked to apply the concept in a new and intriguing way? While rote memorization may have been acceptable (though really it shouldn't be!) in primary and secondary school, it is insulting to ask adults to learn in this manner. Simply talking to a classroom of adults is not continuing education. We expect the people we hire for our companies and who populate our organizations to be intelligent, or at the very least capable of doing their job, so why do we not treat them with confidence and respect when teaching them new skills? A lecture does not show students that they are capable of higher-level thinking and creative output. It only shows them that they are capable of taking up space.

Traditional classes incorporate group work into much of the curriculum, and this has become standard in education on all levels, including colleges and universities. Teams are common in the workplace, and group projects in school are great exercises in experience for the professional world. Teams are small mobs that can create their own learning and sharing systems. When designing work for a team, in a learning situation or in the workplace, it is important to incorporate tasks that require both individual and team effort. Group tasks will appeal more to learners who are focused on active experimentation and those for whom concrete experience builds their knowledge base. Individual tasks that contribute to the group are favored by people who are abstract conceptualization and reflective observation learners. Allowing flexibility within a group of participants to choose their own tasks and plan will give the students a chance to choose the tasks that suit them best. For an instructor, this means crafting assignments that are open, flexible, and allow creativity in both the process and the final product. The overuse of teams can be a problem because it is important to recognize that not everyone learns well and interacts well in a team. This is why there should also be individual tasks that can contribute to the product of the team as a whole.

Limitations of Space, Time, and Products

The physical nature of a traditional classroom setting can itself be a limitation. Classrooms are often designed to be set up lecture style, with the chairs facing a podium. This is changing in some organizations as they seek to place students at round tables spread throughout a room. In a room filled with round tables, there is no classic "front of the room." The instructor is free and able to wander from group to group, while teaching or when the students are engaged in an activity. Teaching spaces should be as flexible as possible, with chairs and desks that can be rolled into different locations and writing boards placed on multiple walls. This physical flexibility means that both students and teachers can adapt their surroundings to the need occurring at that moment. If the students decided to change their facilitation style for the day, they could easily rearrange the furniture to suit their needs. Many of our learning spaces are not flexible, forcing instructors to lecture in a room that sucks the life out of any knowledge by its rigidity. A space that does not allow flexibility is a space that tells both the instructor and the student that they cannot be trusted to choose their own learning environment.

Physical space also limits who can teach and who can attend the learning opportunity. When we are limited by geographical location, only people local to the organization can attend the classes or workshops. Technology has made education, both teaching and learning, accessible to people for whom it was previously an impossibility. Companies and organizations can use technology to have literally anyone teach their members, regardless of where that teacher resides in relation to their organization. This opens up even more opportunities to find instructors in unlikely places and presents the ability for organizations to use technology to develop partnerships outside their boundaries. The internet has wiped away geography as the overriding factor of who could teach and who could learn; those in need of a workshop no longer need to travel miles to a central location. People can learn anywhere, anytime, wherever they are at that moment. It is nothing short of amazing.

Releasing learning from the shackles of physical spaces also results in a large savings for organizations and their members. Physical spaces cost money, to rent the space, furnish the space, heat and cool the rooms, and provide the technology needed to facilitate learning. Providing travel money for employees to go to distant places to learn is a large expense for organizations; these funds are seen as a benefit for professionals who are expected to travel. Some professions expect their members to attend conferences, but do not provide support for this. Virtual classes, workshops, and conferences can be designed, hosted, and attended for a fraction of the cost of a physical class.

A traditional workshop is limited by the constraints of time. It has a distinct beginning and end. When a class is contained within a physical space and time, then the learning itself will have a beginning and an end. Although the teacher may be available after the class for questions, there are few mechanisms for students to continue their learning and reflection after the class is over. For reflective learners, having some time between learning a concept and its application is essential. A traditional face-to-face class gives these learners information, but does not provide an outlet where they can reflect openly and share their ideas within a community. This is another area where the internet has stepped in to heal a fatal flaw in the traditional classroom, providing many communities and tools that can be used to continue the learning experience between teacher and student or student and student, long after a workshop or class has ended. This problem most often applies to workshops or classes in which the instructor and the students meet only once, meet only for a short period of time, or meet in a lecture environment.

Many classes require that students emerge with some sort of product, perhaps a plan to change a process at work, an essay, a new manual for training others, or something that they can take with them to change their professional environment. In a physical classroom, the kinds of products and the forms that they can take are greatly constricted to something physical. A physical object is harder to share widely than a digital product. A single manifesto can be copied and handed physically to a few people, but it can be posted on the web, shared, and read by millions in one day. Very few physical products of learning have this potential for impact in a profession. If technology is incorporated into a class, then the learners could share their reflections on blogs others could read, create videos others could view, or record audio dramas others could hear. After a presentation, the online community, the community outside of the class, would have the opportunity to comment and continue the conversation; the learning does not stop at the borders of the classroom, and the members of the learning community can be infinite. In a traditional classroom, a conversation cannot continue in this same exponential manner because time and space are finite and limiting.

Some classrooms lend themselves to active learning and experimentation, such as classes located in labs, like science or computers. Classes lucky enough to be in a computer lab, or with access to computers and wireless, can integrate technology into the learning environment of the physical class easily, but this access is often contentious. Instructors either see computers in the classroom as a distraction or as a boon to the learning process, and there is a wide variety of each opinion.[5] Some instructors use classroom management systems, which allow the instructor to turn off internet access, lock computers, send surveys out to students, and many other tasks. Some of the features are quite useful and even fun, like the survey feature and the group chat portal. The lockdown feature is what causes the most debate among educators. Some instructors say that locking down a computer prevents vital opportunities to interact in different ways, like on a backchannel, while other instructors see only disengaged students playing around on Facebook. This debate, for the time being, shows no sign of slowing and likely will not until we learn to properly engage students and implement technology in meaningful ways in the physical classroom.

Technology, as the next chapter shows, is not the answer to all problems when educating adults, but it can have real, lasting value in the education process. However, technology use simply for technology's sake is almost always a terrible mistake. A tool should fill a need or solve a problem. Occasionally, a prejudice or ignorance regarding online tools held by the instructor can negatively affect a class. Just as a tool should not be chosen for its shiny factor, in contrast a potential tool should not be ignored simply because of its primary function. For instance, instructors who think that Facebook is a vapid waste of time might fail to see an important application of Facebook in their classes. All solutions should be considered, whether they be low tech (paper and pen) or high tech (podcasting or Twitter). Active learning without technology is done often, but ignoring available tools when they are so ubiquitous in many people's daily lives can be detrimental and destructive.

It is a fact that today's students, and much of today's workforce, are well connected to the ubiquitous web in all aspects of their lives. Their expectations are different because of their ability to be connected anywhere, at any time, with a few clicks of a keyboard or smartphone. A physical classroom has a finite place in time and space and cannot meet all of the needs of the new learner who is always connected to the wide world of information.

Technology and connectedness mean different things to different people, especially along generational lines. The new generation, often called the Net Generation, sees "technologies that are still considered transformative by their parents' and grandparents' standards (for example, instant messaging) [as] a basic part of their everyday lives."[6] Technology is not a computer or the internet; technology is any tool that helps this generation communicate, create, or learn, and they do not see technology as something life-changing. For these students, technology simply *is*. Technology is so ubiquitous that students barely differentiate between the importance of the professor's knowledge of their subject area and the professor's ability to properly and successfully use technology in the course. Not only do they expect the instructor to use technology well, but they also expect technology to be well-balanced with the content of the class.[7] These students expect that technology, as they define it, will be woven seamlessly and effortlessly into their physical learning spaces because it is seamless in their physical lives. Professors and instructors who do not understand this concept will fail to reach their students and thus fail in presenting their love of their discipline to a new generation of scholars. This gap between instructor and student expectations can be devastating.

A learning environment that exists completely in the physical world misses the opportunity to expand into something more and into something that students expect. To a student, technology already exists everywhere and the classroom should not be different. In one study, a whopping 79.5 percent of students said that they learn best with a combination of web searching and lectures.[8] Backchannels, ongoing class discussions, and many, many other opportunities exist for instructors willing to open up their classes in meaningful ways to technology. Technology can be used to integrate different media forms and creative content into a learning environment. Instructors that only see technology as interruptive are missing the potential and the point. Technology does not have to be interruptive to the learning process. It can be used to engage the student and enrich the process. Of course, students in a locked-down atmosphere will see technology as an escape from what they possibly perceive as a disengaged and controlling instructor. Students do still want face-to-face interactions with their professors, regardless of the use of technology: 67.7 percent of students said they would still attend a face-to-face lecture even if the content was placed online.[9] Instructors are still important to students, as is the knowledge they have to impart. Communication and interaction are still highly valued by students even when presented in a traditional setting.

The expectations just discussed all relate to the generations in the halls of higher education now, but they will soon be the employees in our workforce. Even now, our younger employees, and many of our older ones, have some of the same expectations for ubiquitous learning experiences. Once in the workforce, we may attend conferences, go to workshops, or attend staff development days. All of these are opportunities in which the educational experience could be elevated to another level of creativity and interaction. Sadly, much of the continuing education offered to professionals is stuck with the same problems that higher education faces: old style instruction with students in need of a new style of teaching.

Endnotes

1. Anne H. Moore et al., "Learners 2.0? 21st-Century Learners in Higher Education," *Educause Center for Applied Research Bulletin* (April 1, 2008): 6, www.educause.edu/ECAR/Learners20ITand21stCenturyLear/162820 (accessed July 19, 2011).

2. David A. Kolb, *Experiential Learning* (Englewood Cliffs, NJ: Prentice Hall, 1984).

3. David A. Kolb, *The Kolb Learning Style Inventory Version 3.1* (Boston: Hay Resources Direct, Hay Group, 2005).

4. Ken Bain, "What Makes Teachers Great?" *Chronicle of Higher Education* 50, no. 31. (April, 9, 2004), chronicle.com/article/What-Makes-Great-Teachers/31277 (accessed July 19, 2011).

5. Marc Beja, "Promoting 'Netiquette' in the Classroom," Chronicle of Higher Education, The Wired Campus Blog (June 26, 2009), chronicle.com/blogPost/Promoting-Netiquette-in-the/7239 (accessed July 19, 2011).

6. Gregory R. Roberts, "Technology and Learning Expectations of the Net Generation," *Educating the Net Generation*, ed., Diana G. Oblinger and James L. Oblinger (Educause: 2005): 3.2, www.educause.edu/educatingthenetgen (accessed July 19, 2011).

7. Ibid., p. 3.4.

8. Shannon D. Smith, Gail Salaway, and Judith Borreson Caruso, *The ECAR Study of Undergraduate Students and Information Technology*, 2009, Research Study from the EDUCAUSE Center for Applied Research, Volume 6, 2009: 63, www.educause.edu/ecar (accessed July 19, 2011).

9. Ibid., p. 59.

CHAPTER EIGHT

Benefits and Challenges to Leaving the Traditional Classroom Behind

Since the 1980s, computers have increasingly become an integral part of the way we teach, conduct business, and live our lives. The personal computer, in tandem with the internet, has made connecting to others ubiquitous. Few places in the industrial world are not linked to the hive mind that is the internet. Technology has made education more accessible and appealing to a broad range of new students. It has changed the way in which we approach certain disciplines and teaching. This level of connectedness has caused some major changes and expectations in education. It has also increased the gap between organizations that use technology well, and those who implement it badly—or not at all.

Benefits of Leaving the Traditional Classroom

Using internet tools can resolve the issue of physical limitations and geography; an online class does not require a physical venue and can be as flexible as the tools employed in the learning environment. The number of students in an online class is limited by the number of students an instructor can wrangle, not the size of a physical room. An instructor can create an online learning workshop without having to be flown in from another location, so the organization will only have to pay for the time of the instructor, and not the expense of travel. People attending an online class or workshop will not have to pay to travel. Students can interact in many different ways online, sharing many different types of information and media. This kind of sharing is limited in a physical venue by time and resources.

Physical spaces are rarely flexible to the needs of the instructors or the learners. An online workshop can incorporate many different kinds of media and reach multiple learning styles, something that is much harder, though not impossible, to do in a face-to-face class. An online learning environment can easily expand to include tools on the fly, as they are needed. If students decide to implement a new tool for a project, it can be linked to and integrated easily.

Organizations have limited space and funds with which to teach. Even when the economy is not dragging, universities and organizations have to choose between spending scarce education dollars in many different ways. Technology tools can often be implemented cheaply, which is beneficial to organizations that have a small or shrinking continuing education budget. Outsourcing for instructors can be a good solution for some situations, but constantly outsourcing for a talking head will cost more in the long run. Instead, a continuing education program focused on a self-educating mob will spend less money when the collective knowledge held by the group is utilized. Look inward before you seek outside assistance. Physical spaces are costly to create, maintain, and update. Smaller organizations may not have the physical space to accommodate all of the people needing training, and they may not have internal access to a good instructor in the subject needed. Universities are frequently torn between the need for more classroom space and keeping the cost of tuition down.

Organizations are also learning that giving their members flexible learning opportunities means that they can offer more and that people will take advantage of the opportunities in the spare moments they have available. Although still the standard, the 9-to-5 work day is becoming more amorphous as organizations offer a more flexible schedule.[1] Business practices, including training, have also begun to shift to reflect these changes.

Organizations have had to decrease their workforce levels and ask their members to do more work than in the past. This puts time at a premium. Inside an organization, if learning is to take place during the work day, some of the work load should be shifted to accommodate the time needed for each individual to study. If people are required to spend time outside of their normal working hours on continuing education, they should be rewarded or compensated in some way. Some organizations have had success in offering laptops, iPods, and similar items as rewards for people who go above and beyond. This need for a reward is especially important for organizations that don't require employees to complete the training but instead strongly encourage them to do so. Offering incentives is never a bad idea and may make more of a difference than you would think. Though we would like people to want to enhance their learning, most will not put forth a significant effort unless it will benefit them in some tangible way.

Students are increasingly mobile, and they want and need to learn when and where they live their lives. Always-connected learners expect educational opportunities to be constantly available as well. People live in many places online and interact at all hours of the day and night, so students need to be able to learn when it is convenient for them to do so. The internet has made it much easier to juggle other responsibilities in addition to education. Families, careers, and life can now be interwoven with the classroom. The accessibility of education online has made this possible. Organizations and universities must be careful about the time required of students and members for continuing education projects. Universities that offer classes populated by working professionals should be mindful of the fact that these adults returning to school still have full-time jobs and families vying for their attention.

Using online tools to host a learning environment means that learners can access the information when it is convenient for them, so whatever time they have available can become an opportunity to learn. This flexibility appeals to most people and allows more people access to education. A self-paced workshop can be used as a point-of-need education tool or for busy professionals. This type of workshop can be used to answer a question someone has in that moment, which is often a "How do I . . . ?" question, much like an FAQ page but in tutorial or workshop form. A learning-on-demand program lets people from many different time zones participate in the same class without rearranging their lives around a particular time or physical space, so geographically diverse organizations can employ this method to benefit members anywhere, anytime. Learning environments can also be set up with both synchronous and asynchronous events, giving people the opportunity to interact and learn both in real time and when it is convenient. Synchronous events can be used for group discussions or guest speakers, while asynchronous events could be used for archived material, discussion boards, or readings.

As discussed in Chapter 7, everyone has a different learning style. Educational opportunities with online components can include many different kinds of media and learning types. The internet gives any instructor access to thousands of different kinds of tools that have hundreds of different functions; almost any type of media and activity can be woven into a virtual classroom. Students can also create content for their classes in formats that range from the traditional written word to a music video of photos representing a concept. Diversity in learning is always important, in ideas and presentation, so that knowledge can be presented in the way that meets the need of each individual.

The diversity of tools also extends into the realm of learning management systems (LMSs). An LMS is a tool that is used to build a class portal, and these can vary widely. There are proprietary versions, such as Blackboard (blackboard.com), open source models, such as Moodle (www.moodle.org), and tools that are not intended to be LMSs but which have the flexibility to be almost anything, such as WordPress (www.wordpress.org). Although there are few LMSs currently available, you do have some options when creating an online class, ranging from the rigid and terrible Blackboard to a flexible system set up on an open source blog platform. There is more discussion of LMSs in Chapter 11.

Learning that occurs online also has the potential to be much more flexible than a traditional classroom. Gone are the constraints of a physical room. Online, the classroom can be anything from a backchannel on Twitter to a blog post with comments. The classroom online is limited only by the imagination of the learning group and the tools it has chosen. Flexibility in a learning environment also means that the environment is open to change and growth. In a traditional classroom, that means one of three things changes: the instructor, the students, or the physical space in which they meet. Online flexibility means that new tools can be added to the environment at any time. New concepts and modules can be introduced. Different media can be integrated with a few clicks of a mouse. There really is no end to the possibilities.

Classes that incorporate online tools, have an online component, or are completely online have the opportunity to become a learning environment in which the content is largely created by the students. In this kind of environment, the instructor is a guide and the students are free to explore and create. Learning is set up so that the students are not only engaged with the material, but are engaged with each other. They are given the opportunity to respond to the work of their fellow students, to post interesting insights, and to share information they find outside of the class, and they do all of this inside and outside of the physical classroom. The place in which learning occurs is *everywhere*, and students bring back what they find to their classmates. Students in this type of environment feel like they are part of a team and are engaged on levels that are not found in a traditional, lecture-style classroom. Students often engage on a personal level in an environment where they are given the flexibility and safety to do so; what starts out as a disparate group of people becomes a self-supporting learning group, an open creative community whose focus is knowledge sharing.

This new method of exchanging and learning information could be called a knowledge ecosystem. In agriculture, an ecosystem is defined as the interaction between living organisms and their habitat.[2] All the physical factors, including anthropological and societal factors, are taken into account when examining an ecosystem. An ecosystem can include large areas of land or a few specimens, and a healthy ecosystem is self-sustaining and diverse.[3] This definition, when applied to a self-educating mob, works beautifully. A knowledge ecosystem, in its most simplistic form, is the interaction between the students and the knowledge. A healthy knowledge ecosystem would include diverse types of interactions and information, allow for creative communication and sharing among members, be flexible in terms of who and what could be included into the system, and could be a self-sustaining entity, separate from a governing body or individual.

Online tools have created a new level of learning, creating, and interaction that were not possible before.[4] Students can do more, create more, and be more online than they were ever able to in a physical classroom. When given the right tools and flexibility, a class can become something more than a class. It can become a learning journey, a knowledge ecosystem, that is self-sustaining and self-actualizing.

Challenges in Leaving the Traditional Classroom

Unfortunately, all of the problems we have in a physical classroom have followed us into our online learning environments and create new challenges for instructors and students. We have begun to teach each other online, but we repeat some of the same mistakes as in physical classes. The most egregious and common mistake that instructors make is in treating the internet as if it were a physical teaching venue. I believe that there is no single explanation as to why this is so frequent a mistake, when common sense tells us that the internet is not the same as a physical classroom. In many cases, technology is simply used to transmit a traditional-style lecture across a distance. Although this does have some use, a dry lecture in person is just as dry and useless online, and using the internet for straight lectures misses its potential as a learning tool.

There are many ways that online classes can strive to overcome the unique challenges of an online venue, including ways to teach to different styles and incorporate technology, both in a physical and online setting. To utilize technology better, a backchannel or chat between the students and the instructor, which occurs simultaneously with the lecture, can add deep value to the learning process. A simultaneous chat gives the students the opportunity to ask questions as they occur and gives them the opportunity to answer the questions of their peers. A backchannel gives students the ability to explore tangential topics during a lecture with other students while still paying attention to the lecturer. For some students and instructors, this may be distracting, but it can add depth and breadth to a simple lecture. Allowing students to chat and answer each others' questions in this manner will enhance the sense of camaraderie between the students, which will in turn increase the investment the students feel in the class as a whole.

Opportunities for reflective learning increase in an online setting because students and instructors are not constrained by the time limit of a face-to-face class. The delay between the acquisition of knowledge and the following discussion or responsive writing allows time for reflective learners to process the new knowledge, and live chat can be used after a webcast as a discussion group where students can process the information presented. Many online classes also ask students to write reflections on a bulletin board or in a blog. Students will frequently respond to the reflections of others, and in some classes this interaction is required. In this way, the students both create content and respond to the original content of their peers, questioning, commenting, and expanding on the material presented by the instructor.

The first half of this book is dedicated to the idea that the sum intelligence of the whole is greater than the individual. This does not cease to be true when people happen to be in a classroom. A wonderful way to demonstrate acquired knowledge in a subject and to help organize your thoughts is to teach and explain an idea to others, but asking individuals in the class to teach or demonstrate a skill can be invaluable as well. Small groups will have a smaller knowledge base, but they will still possess a wealth of information. Adults who participate in continuing education have had years of experience in their professions and can use their experience to help others learn and enhance their own education. Instructors who work with adults, sometimes called nontraditional students at universities, would be wise to use the knowledge in their classroom to their advantage. Crafting flexible assignments or asking students to be responsible for teaching topics to the class, via a method of their choice are excellent ways to stimulate this kind of learning, creating, and sharing.

Instructors are often asked to teach using technology tools with which they are unfamiliar, and so they are unaware of the true potential of these tools.[5] For instance, most universities and organizations use portals to organize their workshops and classes. An LMS in itself is not a bad framework for a class, but it is usually employed badly, ruining the learning experience for the student and frustrating the instructor. Not only are LMSs implemented in ways that detract from learning, but they are frequently monoliths of inflexibility. For example, a common bad use of a portal involves posting a series of the virtual equivalent of a lecture (or information-heavy PowerPoint lecture), throwing up a bunch of readings, and then requiring students to watch, read, and superficially respond to both on a discussion board. What instructors create here is a portal for busywork, which fails to require the students to explore, reflect, or take any sort of creative ownership over their learning experience.

Alternatively, a good application of an LMS would be to use the portal you create to aggregate data from many different media forms, including audio, video, art, and the written word, in order to present the material in many different ways to your diverse group of learners. Students could then be encouraged to reflect in various ways, using words, audio, or visual media, on what their instructor and peers have posted. They could be encouraged to engage in communication with each other—and with others in the profession who are not directly involved in the workshop or class. Here, practicing professionals can be given access to the class so that they might interact and share with the students, and students should be encouraged to bring in outside sources and share them with their fellow students. There are more ways than a lecture to share knowledge with students.

Universities and organizations that use LMSs tend to offer classes and very large, heavy manuals on the effective use of the system; but few attend, and even fewer implement what they have learned. In a university setting, it is often teaching assistants and research assistants who create the truly nice learning portals. Professors can apply for education grants to create innovative environments within an LMS—which is something that should be done as a matter of course, but making a decent portal in a silo structure like Blackboard takes time and technological proficiency, something that few instructors have at their disposal. Until we teach instructors how to use portals in effective ways to enhance learning, instead of detracting from it, students will continue to have to slog through a process that sucks the fun out of learning. Lack of training for teachers is not a new problem simply because we have added technology to the mix; it has just become more complicated. The tools themselves are a major issue, because the most popular LMS in higher education is Blackboard, a proprietary tool notorious for its poor design and inflexibility. As a graduate student, I had to suffer through semesters in Blackboard and the only thing I learned was how *not* to create an online learning environment.

Making the Most of an Inflexible LMS

If you are stuck using Blackboard or some similar LMS, do not despair of being able to create an interactive and creative learning environment. You can add outside sources and tools to your virtual classroom to enhance the environment for your students. Some tools will be unable to integrate directly into your LMS, but you can place links within the learning space that go out to different places on the web. If the main reason you are forced to use a given LMS is for its grading feature, consider using it only for that and relocate your class into a tool that is more flexible for your needs. Sprucing up your LMS-built classroom relies on three main factors: media, community, and creativity.

Media can add sound, color, and different perspectives to the subject matter. It can be used to introduce a topic or start a discussion. Instead of creating PowerPoint slides, find a video to illustrate the point; it can be inserted into an LMS as easily as a PowerPoint presentation. If you have trouble getting video to sit directly inside your LMS, provide the link to the students. Recent decisions on copyright law have made it easier for educators to include short videos and media in their classrooms. This ruling, made in July 2010, states that it is legal to extract small portions of a DVD for classroom use.[6] If you do not have a hard copy of a video, there are many places online where videos can be searched, posted, and inserted elsewhere. Some of the most popular and interesting are:

- Blip.tv (www.blip.tv)

- Openfilm (www.openfilm.com)

- ScienceStage (www.sciencestage.com)

- Vimeo (www.vimeo.com)

- WatchKnow (www.watchknow.org)

- YouTube (www.youtube.com)

Your school, organization, or company may subscribe to some commercial databases that include videos or are entirely composed of videos for educational use. One such database is called Films on Demand and is produced by the Films Media Group (www.films mediagroup.com). These videos and clips are organized by subject matter and are made to integrate easily into LMSs. Films on Demand is structured so that an individual or a school can subscribe to it. Videos are not the only media available digitally. Music, art, and photos are also wonderful additions to an online classroom. Media of all forms can be found under Creative Commons (www.creativecommons.org) licenses, which often allow for flexible use.

Community in an online learning environment is just as important as the content of the class. Engaged students will feel like the class is part of their community. A community shares and learns from one another; instead of completing their tasks by rote, they will be interacting and sharing new ideas. Learning by discovery has an impact that lectures seldom could, and a vibrant community creates an environment where this type of learning can happen. Most LMS programs have a bulletin board function, but resist the urge to use this as the sole means of communication with your students. Bulletin boards have their place, but other types of communication can enhance the feeling of community. Blogs could replace or supplement your bulletin board, and a tool like Twitter (www.twitter.com) can be used to create a backchannel for a class-room. (For more information on how Twitter can enhance a traditional classroom, see the case study on Twitter in Chapter 11.) A backchannel, discussed in the first section of this book in terms of conferences, can add depth to the conversation going on in the front of the room. Online chat tools can be used for virtual office hours or for virtual class meetings and discussions. A Facebook group for the class allows instructors to communicate with students, and links them together in yet another way.

Creativity has almost no limitations in an online environment. New music, videos, pictures, photos, and reflections can be created online, then shared, discussed, remixed, and shared again. The potential is limitless. Allow students to explore this aspect of creative learning by giving them the freedom to create new content in different media forms for the class. Ask students to post relevant items they find online to the class site. Then, and this is the most important point, let the students discuss their creations and findings with each other openly. These activities permit students to explore and to create the content for the class and to learn from each other. Instead of a class led by the instructor alone, the class becomes a participatory learning community.

There are examples of well-done portals out there, such as a truly amazing portal for an English literature class on Chaucer's *Canterbury Tales*. When I was a librarian at the University of Houston, one of the professors there received an education grant to create a portal for her class. She included interactive maps, videos, and beautiful artwork, and the students were able to become immersed in the stories, the lives of the storytellers, and the daily life of the 14th century. Students took what they had learned and went on a symbolic pilgrimage on their own, either creating a virtual tour, writing their own story, or going through a local contemplation maze. It was the best class I have ever seen set inside the clunky portal environment. This feat of learning was created because the grant money enabled the professor to hire research assistants to create the environment. Creating a great class, physical or virtual, takes time and effort, but we should not have to get grants to do so or hire others to wrangle with the technology. This is not an accessible or long-term solution—though I am sure the Chaucer students appreciated it, and seeing that class made me wish I could be an undergraduate again.

LMSs are not the only instigator of bad teaching online. PowerPoint, the tool everyone loves to hate, has moved its abuse from classrooms and presentation rooms into online learning environments. All of the things that can make PowerPoint painful are compounded when they are "presented" online as a lecture. Cramming as much information as possible onto unimaginative slides and then reading them into an audio file doesn't help anyone learn new information—though you might help them take a nap in front of their computer. Although you might find the sound of your own voice useful, your students are well able to read the slides. Forcing students to follow your pace online is even more excruciating than when it is done in person, unless there is a fast-forward button.

When PowerPoint or similar tools are used, either face-to-face or virtually, it is better if the slides are concise, colorful, and give a broad overview of a topic. Slides are not the place for in-depth explanations of a concept; they are best used as jumping-off points for conversations, broad introductions to concepts, or whimsical looks at topic areas. This rule of thumb works well for lectures and presentations—while many professions pride themselves on jamming as much information on a slide as possible (engineers come first to mind), this is not the best use of the tool. As much as engineers hate to write, they sure like to fill PowerPoint slides with as much detail as humanly possible, and their love of long-winded slides is only eclipsed by their love of colorful graphs. Countless alternatives to PowerPoint are, for the most part, free, innovative, and easily shared with others. Try one of the following tools for something different:

- Prezi (www.prezi.com) is a nonlinear presentation creator that allows comments. Although hard to describe in writing, Prezi is a virtual poster board on which the creator can post almost anything and create a linear video of the path people should follow along the board. It also allows viewers to explore the poster and its ideas in the order of their choosing. This would be perfect for mapping any concept and has some great potential.

- Animoto (www.animoto.com) is a tool that takes photos, videos, music, and text and combines them to create a professional-looking video, which can be downloaded, shared, or remixed.

- 280 Slides (www.280slides.com) is a web-based application patterned after Keynote, the Apple version of PowerPoint. It has all of the flash of Keynote, but does not have to be downloaded onto you computer and is free. Presentations made with 280 Slides can be shared and published in various ways.

- Vokle (www.vokle.com) is a tool that allows you to broadcast live video on the internet and allows the audience to interact with you in real time. This tool includes chat, incorporation of a Twitter feed, and the ability to have the audience ask questions via video.

The other culprit in terrible online teaching is the misuse of webinars or webcasts. Webcasts can be a great online teaching tool, but they often fall prey to the problem that beleaguers other online tools: improper implementation of their possibilities. Webcasts that only include a person talking along with their boring slides are just as useless as a face-to-face lecture with boring slides—only somehow this always seems much more excruciating online than in person. When creating a webcast, always incorporate outside sources. Show what you are talking about, don't tell. This is actually a good principle any time you are teaching, in person or online. If you are discussing a tool, show how the tool works. Go there. Look at it. Do something fun with it. Add some silly music if you are using video.

Be sure to always provide some sort of backchannel for your webcast. Participants should have a way to interact with you and with each other. The backchannel cannot be heralded enough for the value it adds to so many online tools and interactions.

When choosing which tool and how to implement it, always keep in mind the need that tool is meant to fill. Identify the needs of the students, the instructor, and the organization producing the learning environment, and then decide which tool best suits the needs presented. Never, ever choose a tool based solely on its shiny or trendy appeal. It is easy to choose a tool because it is popular and exciting, but tools should always serve a purpose and fill an expressed need. A tool chosen for its sparkly factor may clutter up the learning landscape instead of beautifying it, and too many tools in a learning environment can frustrate students. Each tool may require separate usernames and passwords. If students are required to learn a handful of new usernames and passwords for a single class or workshop they will become resentful before the class even begins. The learning curve for each tool should also be taken into consideration, as the topic of the workshop should never be overshadowed by the students' needs to learn a new technology. The tool should help the learning process, not hinder it.

Technological skill levels will vary among adults in any profession, due to a combination of generational differences, exposure, and inclination. There is no set rule that people of a particular age will or will not be proficient with a technology; never assume that an older person is a technology curmudgeon or that a younger professional is always connected. Generalizations are frequently true, but they are not always—and they could get you in trouble. A wise instructor assumes nothing about his or her students. Those with a low technology skill level will have to learn the technology used in the class in addition to the material, and this can make them frustrated with the process. If the learning curve for the technology is too high, they will not master the tools well enough to explore the subject of the class. These students are often the ones who give up early, drop out, or stop listening. They will need encouragement and perhaps a bit of hand-holding. Students who are proficient with technology will have less to learn, though they may not be familiar with a given tool. When placing students in groups, you might consider pairing people of opposite skill levels so that they can help each other see new things about the tools. Even for a person familiar with the tool, there is always something to learn. A new user might see potential in a tool that a longtime user would miss because of familiarity. (Be aware that this approach may not work with all groups.)

To get a better idea of the skill level of the people attending the class, send out a survey prior to the workshop or class asking about students' familiarity with the tools that will be used. If you know beforehand what to expect, you can better prepare for the people who will need extra help with the technology you have chosen. There are many places to find short tutorials that are under a Creative Commons license, which can be integrated into your learning environment; some of the best ones for basic tools are created by Common Craft (www.commoncraft.com). Tutorials can be helpful for those new to the tool and a good refresher for those at a higher skill level, and you may include tutorials that feature tricks for the more advanced users. In addition to video, there are tutorials available for almost any type of media. Requiring the student to use the tool to complete a simple task is another great way to introduce technology. For instance, if you are using a wiki for the class, ask the students to create their "About Me" page by including some basic information and a picture of their choice.

You can always find multiple tools that serve the same purpose, but with varying cost or customization features. Many can be tested on a small scale for free. Some large-scale tools are free as well, but do require some technical knowledge to run. Other tools are so easy that almost anyone can set them up from beginning to end, regardless of skill level. A simple search on the web will yield step-by-step directions on how to use and customize these tools for different functions, and other sites provide reviews. It is unlikely that you are the first person to be planning a class with the aid of a particular tool. Look for the thoughts of other people online who have traveled a similar road and learn from their mistakes and successes. This is especially true when crafting use guidelines, restrictions, or best practices for your students or your organization. Many organizations have spent significant time on use guidelines for different tools when they are used internally or with the public. It is much easier to use someone else's guidelines as a jumping-off point than to start completely from scratch. The internet makes it possible to share knowledge, and the mob is smarter than the individual: This is as true for tool choice as it is for planning a conference. For a list and description of popular tools, and best uses of various types, please see the Appendix.

The blended classroom has become the most popular form of learning environment in most schools, businesses, and organizations. In this type of class, students do the bulk of their work and interaction online, but still attend a face-to-face class. This blending of physical and virtual usually enhances the knowledge ecosystem of the class. People who only know each other online enjoy meeting in person, and the classroom is no different. When face-to-face interactions are wedded to an online course, it is just as important to keep the spirit of openness and creativity in the physical venue as it is in the online environment.

Management and encouragement of the mob should not be over-looked. A well-nurtured mob that feels like a team will be able to overcome many obstacles. It is important for a class to feel like they are on a journey together, because in a knowledge ecosystem, every-one is important and must contribute to the whole. Students who feel as if they are part of a team will work harder, be more creative, and go above and beyond what they are asked to do for their grade or continuing education points. Chapter 10 discusses best practices and how to manage the mob for optimum productivity and growth.

The addition of online tools into our learning spaces has enhanced the experience when they are used well and assaulted it when they are not. A knowledge ecosystem that exists online has the potential to be rich and vibrant when it includes materials and con-tributions from both inside and outside the official class. The flexi-bility of tools and their integration into the learning process can happen in so many ways that the mind boggles: A mob with the internet at its fingertips has all of the tools, information, and ability to create its own perfect knowledge ecosystem. All they need is some benevolent leadership, a flexible space in which to grow, and the freedom to be themselves.

▶ ▶ ▶ ▶ Going Beyond Blackboard: An Interview with Kyle Jones

Kyle Jones is a PhD student in the Library and Information Studies program at the University of Wisconsin–Madison. He has extensive experience in education, libraries, and building collaborative, creative learning spaces.

How or why did you become involved in education?
My attachment to the field of education has grown over the past eight years, starting back as early as high school during a job exploration program shadowing teachers. I

knew then that teaching and working with students was one of the most honorable and challenging professions; this idea was confirmed as I pursued my secondary education (high school level) certification in English literature and composition during my undergraduate studies. While in the course of these classes and field experiences, I recognized the power of being in such an influential position in students' lives. You find yourself responsible for their futures as you, the teacher, are expected to provide the tools and experiences that will assist their future success.

As I prepped for my student teaching seminar, I was exploring the role of (what were then) newer technologies: blogs, wikis, and the rest of the Read/Write Web change agents. I felt that the avenues and methods for communication and learning provided by these technologies were intrinsic to a higher level of education and a more useful set of skills that extended beyond the school walls. The technologies—blogs in particular—provided opportunities for students to share their work openly with their peers and with the ultimate of authentic audiences: the world. When your work can be read by more than the teacher, there is an unsaid expectation to perform at one's highest ability. It was at this moment that I had my first of many overwhelmingly positive experiences with the open source software WordPress. I deployed its multi-user (WordPress MU or WPMU) version to provide personal blogs for each of my 50 students in two separate composition classes.

In the United States, K–12 public schools are mired in a standards-based educational reform system brought about by the No Child Left Behind Act of 2001. Educational standards, set by each state, require a certain level of performance by pupils. In theory, No Child Left Behind makes sense. In practice, the act has detrimentally affected teacher creativity and reduced the level of integration of instructional technology into the classroom due to its lack of presence in the standards and appropriate funding to purchase some technologies. It is exactly because of this that I left public education after receiving certification and sought out a new profession that was reaching out to technology and understood its influence and need in learners, no matter their age. And so I transitioned into librarianship.

While pursuing my masters in the Graduate School of Library and Information Science at Dominican University in River Forest, Illinois, I was hired at my alma mater, Elmhurst College in Elmhurst, Illinois, as the library information technology specialist at the A.C. Buehler Library. During my tenure at this position, I worked closely with students, librarians, and professors to integrate technologies into their teaching and educational experiences. I also had the opportunity to teach digital literacy classes to English and education majors, classes that were built on my own teaching experiences and research by the Pew Internet and American Life Project and other projects like the *Horizon* report that highlight the importance of technology in education. Being a part of a community of scholars was an important experience for me as a professional and lifelong learner; I somehow knew that academia would lure me back to its campuses somewhere in the future. Little did I know how soon that would be.

After a short time as a knowledge and learning services librarian at the innovative Darien Library in Darien, Connecticut, I returned to the Midwest to be with my family. It was at this time that I was notified of my admittance into the PhD Library and Information Studies (LIS) program at the University of Wisconsin–Madison. The calling back to the classroom came quicker than I thought. My studies are varied, just like I prefer, but are grounded in LIS and instructional technology. I find myself intrigued and motivated as a researcher to look at learning environments, whether officially constructed or organically evolving, to investigate the multitude of ways information is created, exchanged, and modified.

You have designed graduate class portals or LMSs using WPMU. What does this allow you to do that a traditional LMS, like Blackboard, does not?

In my experience with Blackboard as a student and as a liaison for faculty and students, I have found that the rigidity of the system has frustrated professors in online course creation and inhibited learning by students due to discontent with their user experience. Blackboard does many things well. It interacts with systemwide information systems like Datatel; this focus on extensible information has led to the development of a comprehensive grade book (although a difficult component to use). Arguably, Blackboard's structure and lack of flexibility could be touted as advantageous because it provides a level of familiarity for the students from class to class. That being said, Blackboard's closed-door, locked-down philosophy of online learning is not at all relevant in the Read/Write Web society that we engage with outside of the hallowed walls of academia. WordPress is an inherently open system where its flexibility allows administrators—or instructors—to "lock down" portions of the LMS as they see fit. Blackboard acts as the dungeon master to learning; WordPress is the libertarian.

To create these course sites, I have paired WPMU with a relatively new suite of plug-ins called BuddyPress (www.buddypress.org). Taking tips and tricks from the best social networking sites, BuddyPress introduces social and collaborative features like direct messaging, user profiles, forums, activity streams, and groups, among other features pivotal in creating open LMSs. Simply enabling BuddyPress enhances students' options to interact and communicate in ways that would be unwieldy or unavailable in traditional LMSs. Intrinsically, WordPress is a flexible, extensible content management system that is easily molded to a variety of needs; with the addition of BuddyPress, its opportunity for use in learning environments is much more relevant and enticing.

In an interview on the WPMU blog, you said that using WPMU allowed you to change the learning environment based directly on feedback from the students, sometimes

midsemester. Can you give an example of a change they requested that made a difference but which you had not thought of previously?

As the designer of a course's information architecture, look, and feel, you have in mind a certain schema that you believe will seem most logical to the user, the student. You try to arrange the instructor's content so it is easily accessible and makes the most organizational sense. In a closed system like Blackboard this is relatively straightforward. Certain components are set in place and labeled as the software designer saw fit, not by your choice. In a flexible system like WordPress, there is no standard to labeling, way finding, and organization—it is completely up to the mind's eye for what feels appropriate and what has proven successful. This provides an amazingly free opportunity to customize, but also a greater responsibility.

As students began to use the BuddyPress-enabled, WPMU class site, they realized quite quickly through experience with their own course blogs that the platform is highly customizable and extensible. Since they knew full well that the system could be modified to their needs, small requests began to trickle in. In the classes I support, I usually embed myself in a technical support group so students can contact me with any noncourse-related technical questions. Since students know my role—and I advertise myself as "tech support"—requests for tweaks came in the form of homepage adjustments of widgets, plug-ins, and theme installations, and even a system upgrade.

In WordPress, widgets often increase the visibility of recent posts and comments, user activity, and employed taxonomies via tagging and categories, and act as traditional widget-esque activities like pulling in information from outside sources like RSS feeds and any mix of social networks. Widgets can also be rearranged on a page to change their layout. To me, the widget request was technically simple but truly exemplified the necessity of having a customizable system. The students wanted to swap the layout of a few widgets and even remove one that they felt did not assist their learning. They were trying to simplify and improve their experience on the site by making the visible information more meaningful and accessible to them, and these minor adjustments took me less than a few minutes to complete.

As of April 29, 2010, over 9,400 plug-ins and 1,100 themes are freely available from WordPress (www.word press.org/extend). A simple theme change manipulates the look and feel of a WordPress blog, while leaving the content intact. Plug-ins extend the core features of WordPress in myriad ways. The previously mentioned BuddyPress is an exemplary plug-in that demonstrates the potential to change preconceptions of WordPress as just a blogging system. While students were not asking to roll their own social networks, they did request theme installations to customize their blogs to their liking and plug-ins that would further enhance the creation and publication of their content. Theme installations, like widget changes, took very little time and effort on my behalf to enact and I was more than happy to assist in making their learning spaces more their own. At times plug-ins can act closely with the core WordPress system and required me to do a brief offline check of their stability, something I did at my convenience and reported back to the students. Once the plug-ins were vetted, I quickly added them to the installation and advertised the option to use them to the class. While it has become cliché to say "because I can," there's no better way to state how I feel about making these adjustments and enhancements for the students. Students should be able to make their learning experience their own and I feel obliged to assist them.

Why do you feel so strongly that education and the idea of collaborative content creation are linked?

We do not work, live, or learn in silos. Jean Piaget, Lev Vygotsky, and other educational researchers, psychologists, and philosophers used their theory of constructivism to explain how learners create and understand knowledge based on an individual's needs and environments. By way of interactions with peers, communities, and an understanding of self, higher learning is achieved. Vygotsky's work in social constructivism highlights this idea of learning based on environmental context. When students are able to see, read, and interact with their peers' work, they are better able to understand the complexity of the learning task at hand and further their own investigations and self-reflection. This is not by definition "collaborative content creation" since students are not developing works together, but students are engaging with each other's unique works and building understanding due to this open learning environment.

What power does the student have (or should the student have) in today's learning environment?

It is not so much power that students have or should have in their learning environment, but a sense of flexibility and customization. As a student, I achieved more in my learning when I was provided the opportunity to go beyond boundaries of subject material and assignment format; I defined my learning experience. As a teacher, I strive to be the "guide on the side" and not the "sage on the stage," and this is heavily influenced by the tenets of Vygotsky's social constructivism. When students are placed in a supportive learning environment where the boundaries are flexible and the responsibility for their overall success is placed on them, they find ways, like I did, to optimize and customize their learning.

What do you see as the major failing of many instructors or courses today?

I am not convinced that today's instructors have the level of digital literacy that they should to enhance their curricula and prepare students for the obviously techno-centric world they will be members of. This failing does not lie solely on the shoulders of the instructors. Some institutions lack the appropriate technological and personnel resources to assist teachers in refocusing or adjusting their teaching strategies to include digital literacy initiatives. Lowered endowments and funding for higher education institutions cannot act as the scapegoat for not pursuing a higher emphasis on creating digitally literate students when librarians, if instructional technologists and designers are unavailable, have (or arguably should have) the skill sets to provide leadership in this direction.

Is the classroom ruled by the all-knowing professor—the talking head—dead?
No. Some disciplines require teaching methods focused on lecturing and Socratic questioning. However, I would be fearful for the learning of the student if his or her instructor relied solely on lecturing when it was not absolutely necessary. The consummate teacher arrives at such a high level of success by blending a variety of methods and approaches based on the needs of the subject material, the class as a whole, and the individual student.

Do you think crowd-oriented learning environments demand more or less of the students than a traditional class? Do they demand more or less of the instructor?
What I have come to observe with such learning environments is that the influx of information from outside sources and as created by the students themselves is so varied in mode and complexity that there are higher demands placed on both the student and instructor. These demands range from understanding and controlling information overload to being able to effectively communicate in the different modes allowed. For example, an open, online learning environment with an emphasis on social collaboration may provide and encourage these ways for communication: direct, private messaging; group messaging; forum posts; personal, public activity updates (like Facebook); public activity updates (as in posting on another's profile); instant messaging; outside social net-

work communication (like Twitter); personal blog posts; blog comments; and emails. This lists at least 10 varied modes of communication, each requiring different kinds of comprehension, response, and aggregation.

It is quite easy to read this list of increased responsibilities on the students and instructor and write off such a learning environment as a hindrance. And while this example represents the more complex of open learning systems, it does accurately illustrate the complexity of information systems and communication exchange on the web today. Providing a system like this for students prepares them for lifelong learning in what is a decidedly digital information environment.

Why do you think more organizations have not moved to something like WPMU when they are creating learning spaces?

Anecdotally, it seems as if system administrators in higher education are drawn to learning systems that integrate tightly with other software products throughout campus; Blackboard's tie with Datatel is representative of this. Moodle (www.moodle.org), an open source LMS, has over time gained this functionality and is now in greater competition with the Blackboards in education. WPMU lacks these components because it was not developed to be an LMS or have tight integration with other systems. But this is just a system administrator point of view.

Instructional support, a team of which I consider librarians and instructional technologists to be key players, by choice or force, has been tied to Blackboard-esque systems but has tried to fill the gap in its inflexibility with web-based applications like wikis and blogs. Some higher education organizations have, in fact, moved to WPMU in addition to their LMS to provide integral components in online learning that their LMS lacks. Mary Washington University always stands out in my mind as a prime example of pairing WPMU with an LMS successfully. While instructional support teams have understood the value of

WPMU and other Read/Write Web tools, their institutions may not. This lack of institutional support or understanding, I believe, is the major reason for slow adoption in creating learning spaces.

WordPress and WPMU's evolution is just now lending itself to be a comprehensive learning environment as well. While it succeeded above and beyond other systems in providing blogs and open spaces for publication, it was challenging to aggregate the content into an environment that sparked collaboration and supported community building. With the integration of the BuddyPress suite of plug-ins this is no longer the case. The components of BuddyPress are geared toward collaboration, community, and information aggregation in simple and meaningful ways. With its simple administration, extraordinary user experience, and extensible platform, we will in fact begin to see more organizations in and outside of higher education turn to this BuddyPress and WordPress combination to build their own online learning spaces.

What new tool are you excited about now that has potential to impact education?
The quick (and lousy) answer would be to point to WordPress and BuddyPress as an LMS and leave it at that. Ironically, it is not a tool or combination of tools that has the most potential impact on education: It is a change in mind-set. Students, instructors, librarians, and administrators are moving away from picking and choosing Read/Write Web technologies and are refocusing their efforts on the entire learning experience where technology is involved. It is no longer about using a blog, or a wiki, or whatever token technology you choose; it is about the comprehensive package of digital learning—the design, the objectives, the outcomes, the user experience of the system, and so forth.

Endnotes

1. Emily Schmitt, "How a Flexible Work Schedule Can Help You Strike the Balance," *Forbes* (March 16, 2009), www.forbes.com/2009/03/16/work-life-flextime-leadership-careers-flexible.html (accessed July 19, 2011).

2. Neil A. Campbell et al., *Biology: Concepts and Connections* (San Francisco: Benjamin Cummings, 2008).

3. "Kids Corner: Definition of Ecosystems," Michigan Technological University School of Forest Resources and Environmental Science, forest.mtu.edu/kids corner/ecosystems/definition.html (accessed July 19, 2011).

4. John Seely Brown and Richard P. Adler, "Minds on Fire: Open Education, the Long Tail, and Learning 2.0," *Educause Review* 43, no. 1 (January/February 2008), www.educause.edu/EDUCAUSE+Review/EDUCAUSEReviewMagazine Volume43/MindsonFireOpenEducationtheLon/162420 (accessed July 19, 2011).

5. Anne H. Moore et al., "Learners 2.0? 21st-Century Learners in Higher Education," *Educause Center for Applied Research Bulletin* (April 1, 2008): 3, www.educause.edu/ECAR/Learners20ITand21stCenturyLear/162820 (accessed July 19, 2011).

6. James H. Billington, "Statement of the Librarian of Congress Relating to Section 1201 Rulemaking," U.S. Copyright Office, www.copyright.gov/1201/2010/Librarian-of-Congress-1201-Statement.html (accessed July 19, 2011).

CHAPTER NINE

Creating Your Own Knowledge Ecosystem: Harnessing the Power of Mob Labor

Continuing education does not have to be costly for either organizations or employees—when you look in the right places for instructors and tools and allow your mob to create its own knowledge ecosystem. The following sections outline ways for organizations to enable their own mob rule learning. Note that throughout this chapter and often in the second half of the book, I discuss "members" of organizations. I am using this term loosely to encompass both individual members of organizations and employees of companies, as "members" is a more inclusive and general term than employees.

Assessing the Needs of Your Organization

Before you begin assessing the skills and abilities of your members, you need to assess the educational needs of your organization. These needs should align with the direction in which the organization is, or would like to be, going. Often these needs are identified through a strategic directions process. There are many ways to ask individuals within an organization what they think they need to know or what they would like to learn. Here are a few simple examples:

- Send an organization-wide email that people can reply to and possibly discuss among themselves.

- Put members in a room together and ask them to brainstorm about what they would like to learn.

- Brainstorm as part of a standing meeting and repeat this process for different working groups.

- Send out an online survey (which can be collated with less work than an email), flip charts, or other lower-tech methods.

- Ask managers and committee chairs what needs they see within their working groups.

- Ask organization members what needs they see in their peers.

As always, giving members the ability to participate in the process gives them a feeling of ownership and investment in the results. If you are trying to move your organization in a different direction through education and skill training, then you will need the goodwill of your members to be successful. After a needs assessment has been done, the next step should be an assessment of the skills and abilities of the individuals of the organization. The challenge often lies in identifying the skills of your members and matching them with the needs of the organization.

Assessing the Skills of Individuals in the Group

Identifying the wealth of skills held within an organization can be done either informally or formally. Informal information gathering, like talking to people and asking questions, can be done at any time but is often hard to quantify, and even harder to document. The goal in searching out the skills of members should be to create some sort of organization-wide knowledge base or log that can be accessed at any time. Gathering informal data can be difficult but is not impossible. If going about information gathering informally, both managers and peers in the organization should be queried, and the process should be done as unobtrusively as possible. This should not be presented as more work to do but rather as an opportunity to brag about the skills of peers and the organization as a whole. A formal process, followed up by informal information updates, is a great place to start.

Formal skill assessments can be done through surveys or other self-identification methods. Skills can be listed as part of the annual review process and gathered with other materials. A survey can be easily crafted with online tools; see the Appendix for a list and descriptions of a few popular tools. Using a survey tool allows you to easily display and collate answers, which will be especially helpful if your organization is large. Include both open-ended and multiple choice questions. If you have a list of needs for your organization (and you should), you can use that list as a basis for the multiple choice questions, and then use open-ended questions to let people identify their own skills and interests. Open-ended questions may reveal some unexpected but valuable skill sets among your members, so encourage people to list skills and interests outside of their normal job duties. These questions might be the most important and necessary in the long term, as outside skills will be especially useful if you are looking to grow your members and organization in new directions.

Many people have highly developed outside interests, and any individual may be an amateur enthusiast in an area that can benefit your organization. In *Crowdsourcing*, Jeff Howe talks about how the idea of the amateur has changed over the past century to reflect something negative.[1] He begins by explaining that in Greek, amateur means lover. Someone who loves is also passionate. A little more than a hundred years ago an amateur was considered an expert in a field, though it may not have been his chosen profession. In fact, most amateurs were wealthy men of leisure who had time to develop and research their interests. They were the true scientists and thinkers of their day.

Today, we unfortunately guard ourselves against amateur status. We have gatekeepers in every profession and have forgotten that some of the most passionate people in a field of study are the ones who have chosen it out of love. The fact that people explore an interest outside of their jobs does not mean that they cannot be extremely useful and wealthy sources of information. For example, you may have someone who works at a service point in a company, but who has a lot of experience with photography and photo blogs. If your organization is considering a photo blogging project, this unlikely staff member may be the perfect individual to help others within the organization learn to take pictures and post them online. Giving responsibility to people in an area they enjoy shows a deeper understanding of these individuals, and those who know their organization and pay attention to it will want to invest more in the organization that is investing in them. Amateurs are the reason that you must always consider outside interests when assessing the skills and knowledge within your organization.

There are problems with having people self-identify their interests; in particular, people will frequently over- or underestimate their skills.[2] For obvious reasons, both can be problematic if you need an accurate list of the knowledge held within your organization. This problem can be tempered by gaining experience with members of the organization and learning their personality tendencies. People often inflate their abilities out of ignorance, not arrogance. They do not know what they do not know.[3] This inability to identify areas in which you lack knowledge makes self-assessment troublesome, but there are some ways to combat this. In addition to a self-assessment, members could be asked to identify other people within the organization that they think are knowledgeable about certain areas. Peers are often more aware of others' skills or interests than managers or others in upper levels of an organization. Combining a formal survey of skills augmented by informal assessments of peers will create a more complete picture of your organization's skill set.

Finding Instructors in Unlikely Places

After you have identified the needs and the knowledge within your organization, the next step is to find instructors and teachers within the organization. The members of your organization, a mob unto themselves, are likely hiding some instructors waiting to be discovered, but the people holding the skills and knowledge that need to be shared across the organization often lack experience teaching others. If this is the case, then there are some options for using these untried individuals in different ways. People with no formal teaching experience, but with some teaching skills, may be willing to learn how to teach. The first question to ask is, "Is this person a natural teacher?" Some people have the gift of teaching. They are comfortable teaching or talking to groups. Although teaching may not be a part of their formal job description, these people like sharing what they know and may often teach their peers informally in conversations. Most natural instructors are good with people; it is rare to find a true introvert who is a great instructor. Natural teachers can explain concepts using various approaches, helping others see different ways to accomplish tasks, or simply to help others learn the subject on the understanding level of the individual. These naturals can be asked to develop a class or workshop on a subject they know well. It may be a pleasant change for them from their regular routine. You should examine each and every individual, looking at everyone as a possible mine of precious information waiting to be refined and displayed.

Your organization may already have within its ranks people with teacher, trainer, or instructor as part of their job description. You can use them in a few different ways to fill internal education needs. If you are lucky, those with the knowledge that you need will already be teachers, and you can ask these members if they would be willing to teach new subjects that match the needs you have identified. If your organization has experienced teachers in its ranks, they can also be employed to "train the trainer." Training the trainer from within your ranks is another great use of the knowledge and ability of your mob. Every good trainer has tips and skills that they can teach others. Pairing an experienced trainer as a mentor with a new teacher is a wonderful way to empower individuals and to grow the skills in your organization. If your goal is to create a self-sustaining knowledge ecosystem, dispersing the teaching responsibilities and abilities throughout the mob is essential to its growth.

Training the trainer can be done by using members who are not necessarily instructors or teachers. Your organization may not have anyone who teaches internally as a formal part of his or her job, but you may have some individuals who give workshops or speak at conferences. These people are teachers in their own way, and you can use them to help train others to speak and teach. One of the hardest things to learn as a teacher is how to talk and connect to groups, but people who present successfully in other venues can transfer these skills to a smaller classroom. Good speaking skills and hands-on demonstration are the prerequisites for a basic workshop. As discussed earlier, giving presentations at conferences does not mean you are a good teacher. When choosing an instructor to train your group, it is beneficial to have first seen the person in action, which will give you a solid foundation to judge the quality of his or her teaching. If you are not able to attend a session beforehand, ask around and see how those who have seen the prospective teacher feel about his or her abilities.

Training trainers within your organization has two important outcomes. Since the organization does not have to spend money to find outside trainers, that money can be spent elsewhere. However, if you do have to spend some money to train your trainers, this should be seen as an investment. Trainers can always learn new things to share with others. Investing in individuals shows them that they are important to the organization. This investment breeds loyalty and a willingness to work toward the goals of the organization. Members who are loyal are more likely to stick around and be helpful innovators. More trainers means a larger pool of skills and knowledge from which to draw.

Training your trainers also has an interesting side benefit. Once members have some experience teaching others a subject, they can also teach others to teach. Then, those people gain some experience, and they can teach others, and so on—until everyone who wants to be a trainer is a trainer of some kind or another. This is one sign of a healthy and growing knowledge ecosystem; it has the ability to expand with the needs and changing skill set of its members, because there are many teachers available. Many people have the ability to teach others, in small or large groups, but we do not always think of teaching individuals. We should. Imagine if your entire organization were populated with people who were both passionate about your organization and had the ability to teach others that passion. Searching for someone with both the knowledge needed and the skills to share it would require nothing more than sticking your head out of your office.

Consider the skills of each trainer. Some people are great with either large or small groups. These are your natural or experienced teachers, for which the size of the group does not matter, only the subject shared. Some instructors are better with smaller groups or facilitating discussions, but are terrified of larger groups. This is all right, because hands-on workshops can be executed well in smaller groups; hands-on learning requires an active teacher who has time to interact with each student. Active learning in hands-on workshops is often carried out on a small scale because the classes can be constrained by the physical space available. If a computer lab, for instance, only has 10 computers, you will only be able to hold classes for 10. Following a hands-on workshop with a discussion session can keep ideas fresh and supply new ways to employ the skills learned. Many instructors who prefer smaller groups will also be more comfortable teaching classes on technology tools. Showing how-to's and tricks for a technology tool they know well may be easier than addressing a large audience.

Encourage your members, though, to grow outside of their comfort zone in terms of teaching peers and training themselves and others. Even one-on-one training should be valued and encouraged: If one person trains one or two people, then those two can train one or two people, and so on. Soon you'll have a large number of people who have shared information and have gained skills. No formal training is required for this method, which also has the advantage of built-in mentoring opportunities. (There is, however, little quality control with this sort of informal one-on-one training.)

Looking for new trainers internally is a great way to grow organizations, but be wary of empowering people who are not good teachers to go out and teach. Everyone has had an excruciating class—either in school or in a professional setting—and the unfortunate part is that your feelings about the subject were likely (however inadvertently) affected by the bad instruction you received. A teacher has the ability to influence how the learner feels about a subject, and learners will more successfully acquire skill sets if they're excited about the skills they are learning. These skills should be seen as valuable, useful, and, hopefully, fun, and a good teacher will go a long way toward making that happen. Hold instructor evaluations after all formal teaching sessions. Like skill assessments, evaluations should have both open- and closed-ended questions, allowing individuals to rate the knowledge gained and the instructor's ability. These evaluations should not be used to punish, but rather to keep markers on how instructors can improve the ways they teach others.

One way to keep new instructors from conducting disastrous training sessions is to first have them give a practice class to a set of instructors. (If you cannot wrangle two or more instructors for a "class," then honest and cooperative volunteers will work as well.) It is important that these volunteers are willing to give helpful feedback. Have the instructor give the class as though it were real. Then the "students" can offer feedback and comments on the performance. After one practice session, the new instructor can take the feedback and make adjustments as needed. The practice students should particularly make notes on:

- What was unclear about the explanations?

- Did the instructor tell more than show? Explain your response and provide an example.

- Was the pace of the class OK? Too fast? Too slow? Not going too fast during demonstrations is especially important.

- Did the instructor ask the class good questions?

- Did the instructor ask for some kind of participation?

- Did the instructor leave out anything important?

- Did the instructor explain all the steps? Even the simple ones?

- Did he or she make eye contact?

- Could you hear the instructor clearly?

- If the instructor used slides or other visuals, were these helpful, distracting, boring, or something else?

Smaller organizations face different challenges than larger organizations. In a large organization, the problem is finding talent hidden in a large pool. In smaller organizations, the mob is smaller, and thus their combined knowledge is smaller. This does not mean that smaller organizations cannot employ some of these methods; it is just as beneficial, perhaps even more crucial, for smaller organizations to know exactly what their talent pool holds. The problem is that the pool is less likely to cover all of the needs of the organization. To fill the gaps in the expertise of your mob, you may need to look outside of your borders.

Knowledge Sharing

Most organizations are already in some kind of partnership with other entities that can help provide training or teachers. Small nonprofits are usually part of a group of nonprofits that support each other. Small business owners frequently join small business groups that offer moral support for challenges that only small businesses face. Some organizations, like libraries or other public interest groups, are members of consortia. Many of these groups offer classes and workshops to members, and, if your group does not currently do so, perhaps this is your opportunity to spearhead a new project for others in your area.

Pooling resources—expanding the borders of the mob—increases the chance of finding the diamond you're seeking. Resources can be in the form of knowledge held by individuals, companies and organizations, physical space, or monetary resources. Another organization may have a teacher who can train new trainers in other groups. There might be nonprofits in your area that have integrated social media into their fundraising schemes successfully; ask them if they are willing to hold a workshop for other nonprofits and share what they have learned. A larger organization may be willing to sponsor a learning opportunity for new start-ups in the area. A group with ample space could donate the use of its rooms for an unconference or other gathering. This sharing of information can take place in person or in an online venue where everyone is encouraged to participate, so think outside of the physical limitations about the kinds of sharing that could occur within a community. There are endless ways to share knowledge among the members of a large community.

For-profit businesses and more proprietary organizations may be more likely to resist efforts to share resources in this fashion. Secret keeping is standard operating procedure for most businesses, but it does not have to be. James Surowiecki tells stories of geographically and organizationally diverse groups of scientists, mainly in the context of the Human Genome Project, who worked together toward a common goal.[4] Research companies often hold secrets so tightly that few of them ever see the light of day. However, by sharing information and working separately on many different parts of the same question, research and knowledge, like mapping the human genome, have increased, and the productions of the companies have increased as well. Breakthroughs in medicine and modern genetics happened because individuals and organizations released control of information and worked together. Sharing information and transparency did what keeping secrets never could have accomplished.

Organizations can benefit from the wealth of knowledge held by the mob online, where much of the sea of information on every topic imaginable can be harvested to create an online learning environment of your own. Using information created under a Creative Commons (CC) license that allows for sharing is a great way to develop an online workshop. Some customization may be needed, but there is no need to reinvent the wheel. Look for videos, audio recordings, journal articles, slide shows, and many other things that can be pooled together as resources for the members of your organization.

Most CC licenses simply require acknowledgment and a link to the original creator, while some allow remixing, additions, or changes to the original content. A self-paced online learning environment is a perfect option for organizations whose members will be learning on their own time or at various times throughout the day. When it is too complicated to gather everyone together physically, creating an online learning environment is a wonderful alternative.

Consider creating a learning program with modules, with each module as its own topic, so that people are free to complete only the modules that apply to them. Over time, modules can be added from outside sources or created from within the organization, resulting in an evolving knowledge ecosystem supported on many levels of the organization.

Maintaining the Knowledge Ecosystem

After a learning mechanism and system is in place, frequent assessments of the condition of your knowledge ecosystem are required for continued healthy growth. The mob and instructors should be queried often about how the learning experience is going. Although formal assessments are important, such as surveys after workshops or at the end of a module, use some informal methods for collecting data as well. If you are building an online learning community, have a discussion area for suggestions and improvements. Ask members questions like:

- What topics would you like added to the list?

- What topics have become outdated and need to be removed or updated?

- Is there a better way to present the topic than what is being currently done?

- Is there a better tool that we could be using to do X?

- Is there something that you would like to teach the community that you think would be useful?

- Is the current learning environment meeting your needs?

- What other capabilities would you like to have as a learner? As an instructor?

Within the discussion area, members should be allowed to post suggestions and discuss the suggestions of others. This should not be a one-way conversation. Transparency in the process is important in mobs and this is no exception. Allow an open area for discussion in which members feel comfortable brainstorming and applying constructive criticism.

A knowledge ecosystem should be built on tools that can be easily edited and added to by members of the community. The tool that is chosen to house the collective knowledge and resources of the group will make a large impact on the experience of the individuals and the organization, so it should be chosen for its flexibility. The mob may, and probably will, take their knowledge ecosystem to unexpected places, so members should have a tool that can grow with the system. Tools should also be chosen based on their ease of use. Some mobs will need the easiest tool available—and a lot of extra help using even that. Some communities will be able to build their own tools. Keep your groups in mind when choosing a tool for them. Some groups may have enough technology knowledge and background to choose their own tools, so consider asking, instead of telling, what tools they would like. Finally, tools should be chosen based on the cost and the support that comes with that cost. Some tools have no IT support and some do but you have to pay for the help. Your organization and its finances will decide what kind of budget your learning projects will have. For a longer discussion of the types and tiers of technology tools, read the Appendix.

Sometimes an individual's need for new education opportunities will exceed the organization's abilities. Like organizations, individuals seeking education opportunities can rely on the mob to meet some of their needs. Simply being affiliated with an organization, especially a professional one, may grant you some learning opportunities. Many organizations—and thus their members—also have benefits through consortia and related business groups. Professional organizations offer workshops and conferences to individual members at reduced rates and occasionally for free as part of membership. Companies will frequently subsidize the cost of professional organization membership or continuing education. Some companies will even pay for their employees to seek higher degrees in return for extended years of service, an indentured servitude in exchange for education.

Individuals can also find self-paced learning options online, although the sheer volume can be overwhelming. To avoid information overload, start out small. Find a handful of blogs or online journals on the topic of your choice and make reading them a daily or weekly habit; or listen to podcasts if you need your hands and eyes free for other tasks. You can subscribe to a podcast in much the same way that you subscribe to a blog, and listen to it on an MP3 device or right on your computer.

Education and training are vital to the growth of an organization and its members. It may seem like a hefty investment to grow trainers and a knowledge ecosystem from within your own organization, but this quickly pays for itself. Employers need to consider giving their employees time to learn and share with others. An organization whose members seek opportunities to grow is an organization that itself evolves and grows. Transparency within the organization and between organizations can develop a larger system of knowledge sharing that benefits the multitude. Organizations should apply significant time and resources to the care and feeding of their mob and empower their mob to invest in the community at large. This is how organizations become leaders in their fields.

Endnotes

1. Jeff Howe, *Crowdsourcing: Why the Power of the Crowd Is Driving the Future of Business* (New York: Crown Business, 2008): 84.

2. Tori DeAngelis, "Why We Overestimate Our Competence: Social Psychologists Are Examining People's Pattern of Overlooking Their Own Weaknesses," *American Psychological Association* 34, no. 2 (February 2003), www.apa.org/monitor/feb03/overestimate.aspx (accessed July 19, 2011).

3. Steve Schwartz, "No One Knows What the F*** They're Doing (or The Three Kinds of Information)," The Blog of Steve Schwartz, jangosteve.com/post/3809 26251/no-one-knows-what-theyre-doing (accessed July 19, 2011).

4. James Surowiecki, *The Wisdom of Crowds* (New York: Anchor, 2005), Kindle ebook: Location 2539–2542.

CHAPTER TEN

Planting, Caring For, and Feeding Your Mob

Moving an educational program from a teacher-focused class to a self-taught mob is a paradigm shift that will likely be met with trepidation, or at least many questions. We have relied on experts for so long that we have forgotten how to value collective knowledge. Changing the way things are commonly done means changing people's ideas about what is possible and about the valid methods for a learning process. The larger an organization, the harder this shift may be. The first half of this chapter discusses ways to overcome the obstacles that will keep your mob's learning environment from being successful, including resistance, challenges, and follow-through. The second half lists some best practices for both organizations and individuals to help nurture and grow your mob. Though this section of the book discusses many different kinds of adult learning environments, this chapter is mostly applicable to learning scenarios in a work or other large organizational setting. However, some of the information on fostering healthy, successful self-educating mobs will be useful in many situations, in and out of a learning environment.

You can encounter resistance any time the word *change* is involved. Although some people thrive on change and challenges, many view change with some degree of wariness. Our initial reaction is to avoid change, even though it is a constantly occurring phenomenon. When you are dealing with just one person, resistance to change can be overcome directly. But, when you multiply one person's resistance throughout an entire crowd of people, fighting an amorphous enemy can be exhausting. There are ways to guide a group through change with less pain for everyone involved. (Note that there will always be people who will need to be dragged kicking and screaming toward any form of change!)

Resistance to change almost always boils down to one thing: fear. This is manifested in many ways other than an actual display of fear, running the gambit from anger to indifference. Instructors may fear that a self-educating mob will no longer need them and thus they will lose their position. Organizations may fear the unknown: How does a self-educating mob function in a chaotic environment? Individuals may fear their own lack of knowledge and ability to contribute to the whole. If you understand where the fear originates, then you can try to address it.

Providing education and information about the shift from teacher- to mob-centered learning is a good first step toward combating this fear. An atmosphere of open information goes a long way toward dispelling fear of the unknown. This is one reason transparency is so important—and the discussion of transparency has taken on a different kind of urgency since the internet has made secret keeping virtually impossible. Some level of online exposure will be forced on organizations that do not practice transparency, and forced exposure is rarely good exposure. It is much better to simply be open and transparent from the beginning with the workings of your group and its deliberations.

Transparency is not easy for most large organizations. It goes against standard operating procedure. Don Tapscott says, however, that, "Our research shows that transparency is critical to business partnerships, lowering transaction costs between firms and speeding up the metabolism of business webs. Employees of open enterprises have higher trust among each other and with the firm, resulting in lower costs, better innovation, and loyalty."[1] Transparency is beneficial for the financial and mental health of an organization. If you want to make changes in how people learn and share knowledge in an organization, be open with them about what you want, what you are trying to do, and how you would like to do it. You may be surprised at the innovative ideas your mob can contribute when they are asked openly.

▶ ▶ ▶ ▶ ▶   ## An Example of Problem Solving With the Mob

Your organization needs to have a method in place to train members that would allow them to progress through training at their own pace and eventually create new online workshops for others. You would like to implement some sort of course management program, like Moodle (www.moodle.org). There are multiple issues with implementing a new system, including technology support, managers allowing time for training to occur throughout the day, organically growing new modules from members themselves, training on the new tool, and the simple willingness of each individual to participate in the project.

So, you call an open meeting that everyone is invited to attend. The idea—that members become responsible both for their progression through the education system and that they would eventually create new modules for each other—is laid out before them. The members are asked to decide how they would like to discuss the issues. The facilitator gives some ideas and steps down, and the group members then choose a discussion path. Perhaps they decide to discuss the benefits first. Or, perhaps they make a list of challenges to the proposal and then proceed to suggest solutions to the challenges posed. The group may also make a list of topics it would like to see eventually included. Modules could be added or created right away. This discussion will likely need to take place over more than one meeting.

In this example, the facilitator talked very little and the individuals were allowed to take over the process. The mob took control of the direction of their learning. If managers or people perceived to hold the power dominate the process too much, separate discussions may need to be held, with those in power in a different discussion group than those without. After an initial separate session, the two groups can be brought back together for joint sessions. Although the mob may need some facilitation guidance—a benevolent dictator—it will not benefit from one already powerful individual asserting autocratic power over the group.

There are many ways to introduce an idea slowly on many fronts while asking for continual input and feedback. Repeated exposure to an idea breeds familiarity and can eventually foster acceptance. Repeated exposure is in itself a method of education. Giving people the opportunity to discuss new ideas and to change in informal settings fosters transparency, and all the benefits that entails, and it also gives people a chance to reflect on the ideas over time. Brown bag discussions or a meeting run with an Open Space Technology facilitation style can be a nonthreatening way to introduce a new idea. The beauty of these methods is that the group in attendance, the mob, can take the idea and then discuss it in whichever direction they choose. The facilitator for the gathering is responsible only for introducing and explaining the topic; the discussion can then be turned over completely to the people. Mobs given some power to go their own way can solve many of their own problems through discussion and exploration.

Large-scale discussions, although often the best option when promoting an idea with transparency, do not work in every situation—and sometimes you may not be in a position to schedule such discussions. If you are not in a position of power within an organization, you can still be in a position of change. When working from the bottom or from the middle, converting allies, advocates, and fans to a belief in the wisdom of the mob may be the best way to start. Talking with individuals one on one and explaining the benefits of a self-educating mob may be the only option to you at the beginning. The goal should be to win not just allies, but fans of your idea. Allies may agree with you, but fans will actively seek to advance your cause. Fans have passion. Fans will spend their own time converting others to the benefits of education by mob. Fans have ideas that can trickle into a renewed passion for the profession as a whole. Enthusiasm for the profession that stems from the belief that every individual has something meaningful to share with the group will nurture the health of the mob. However, passion is not just for members of a profession or professional organization. Passion can be held by employees for their company or by members of a class. What would your company look like if every member cared about your mission and product? How much more creative learning would occur in your classroom if your students were passionate about the subject? It is easier to change the world with an army at your back than to be one lone person yelling into a canyon.

Resistance to using the mob to self-educate may come from the people who hold decision-making power in the organization. Those in power have to consider many different aspects of a situation, so provide them with as much information as you can to show them the benefits of what you are proposing. Find examples of how other organizations, similar to yours if possible, have used crowd-centered education. Use these examples as a jumping-off point to show ways that you may adapt these ideas to make them better fits for your organization. Notice what did not appear to work well in practice at other organizations, and make the necessary adjustments. When talking with managers, be transparent about these adjustments and the problems with the original idea. They may have some suggestions to improve the system, given your organization's specific needs and resources.

When talking with decision makers in your organization, emphasize the return on investment (ROI). ROI is the amount of benefit received from a service, product, or action when compared against the cost of the item. The ROI for a mob that self-educates can be very high in ways that are sometimes unexpected. Finding new teachers and fountains of knowledge within an organization creates a system where individual members feel appreciated, and where those individuals are contributing to the health and education of the group as a whole. Individuals who contribute and feel that they are part of a larger team, a mob, will also be more loyal to that group, organization, or company. Loyalty is what fans feel, and every organization should strive for the passion of fans. More tangible returns on this system could also include decreased money spent on outside instructors and travel costs. Training money could be reserved for instances where outside training was truly necessary; instead of outsourcing every training need, a mob could be asked to provide the leadership and training. Most of the costs associated with a self-educating mob lie in the tools that are chosen to facilitate communication if using technology-based spaces, or the maintenance or rental fees associated with physical spaces if physical venues are used.

Organizations are often unwilling to risk immediate large-scale implementation. Small-scale, low-risk trials can be a proving ground for a great idea. If there is already a small working group or committee within your organization, consider using it as a guinea pig for a self-educated group. Invest time and effort into the group members to help them be as successful as possible. Keep in mind that if you choose to employ this method, smaller groups also have a smaller knowledge base from which to draw. It might be necessary to team up with similar groups in other organizations to increase the knowledge pool of your mob. Swapping instructors and ideas with another organization can benefit both these smaller groups and your organization as a whole.

Small-scale implementations will have small successes and small failures. If the idea fails, then you have lost little but time and pride. If the implementation is flawed in some way, you can fix the flaws when moving the system to a larger group. Failure should not be seen as something negative; mistakes should be seen as learning opportunities. They are opportunities to take what was done wrong and make it right, and to start again doing something better than before. Small successes should be built upon, heralded, and shouted from the rooftops. Always use successes to win over more people and prove the worth of an idea. Successes can be used as a foundation to build something new and exciting.

If you are seeking to incorporate technology into your knowledge ecosystem, look for tools that have free trials. Paid versions of tools will often have extra bells and whistles, but the trial version will give you an idea about what the tool can do, what it can't do, and how usable the tool is in real life. Ask your mob to test the tool and get feedback. Be honest about what you would like to do with it. Transparency with crowd members is always advisable when you want them to work with you in an endeavor. If the tool does not work as you would like, then you have lost nothing but some time. The process of evaluating a tool as a group may allow individuals to express needs that have been previously unvoiced. Be cautious, though, about spending so much time testing or debating that you do not actually make any significant decisions that move the group forward. This may be a back-end way to get groups talking about what they feel their education needs are and how to address them.

You may not have other uses and examples of the tools you want to use because you have come up with an entirely new way to share knowledge within your mob. If this is the case, you may be able to share the innovation angle with the people in power in order to gain their blessing. Being the first organization to do something innovative can be rewarding, if scary and uncertain. Some organizations do better with this type of change than others.

When all else fails, subversion is another tried and true way to effect change. Subversion, the opposite of transparency in many ways, is a means to do what you want despite opposition. Subversion involves implementing your idea in small, subtle ways (or sometimes not so small), and proving its worth through success. When choosing the subversion route, keep in mind that successes may need to be grand in order to win over naysayers. Subversion is also known as asking for forgiveness rather than begging for permission. At times it is easier to plead a mea culpa than beg until blue in the face for permission.

Resistance that occurs on the bottom of the organizational pile stems from different reasons. Some reasons are the same, like a fear of change, but for many it will hinge on their place as a cog in the system. For cogs, change can be reduced to how things specifically affect their job or work flow. The fear is either that their duties will increase without comparable time to accomplish them or that their duties will not exist under a new system. If people are expected to learn new skills and apply them to their work flow, they must be given time in which to do these things. It sounds obvious, but far too often we ask people to take on more responsibilities without giving them adequate time in which to complete the new tasks. In a work setting, all the managers need to be supportive of learning initiatives or you will end up with a working group whose manager demands that they complete the training because the organization said they must, but who will not allow time for their workers to learn. This creates resentment on many levels and becomes frustrating for those without power within the organization.

To create an environment where members are given time and encouraged to complete training, organizations should set aside reasonable amounts of time for education, there should be transparency during the process, and members should be asked what they want to learn. The collective knowledge of the mob, as we have discussed throughout this book, is greater than the small handfuls of committee chairs or managers. Organizations as a whole will be able to suggest new training for themselves and their peers. Transparency in the process and open discussion will allow people to feel comfortable suggesting new topics for training. Within the organization, there may be smaller groups that are able and willing to create learning modules on these topics for their peers.

Training programs often fail to deliver results when it comes to maintaining momentum from a training workshop, the integration of new skills, and the maintenance of the new skills. If you are creating a learning environment for the members of your organization and you want the members to actually participate, you should offer incentives to do so. Although we want people to be driven to learn and achieve simply for their own edification, this is not the case with most people. They need to be given a compelling reason to set aside time in their already busy day to learn and use a new skill. Simply requiring training may promote completion of the program but it will not promote involvement and passion in the process. Some organizations that have asked their members to complete a long training program have offered MP3 players or computers as rewards for completion. People simply want their time acknowledged as precious and to be rewarded for a job well done.

New skills learned during a training workshop should be integrated into the normal work flow of the organization. A skill acquired but not utilized is a skill lost. If the skill learned is a building block to other skills, then continued building of skills is a way to synthesize what has been learned. Application of new knowledge is a higher level learning skill than simple acquisition. Members who have acquired skills can also be asked to train other people within the organization. Teaching others is another higher-level learning skill that forces the instructors to synthesize and examine the information they have acquired. Organizations that train their members and then ask those members to train others will establish a system where the mob can seek knowledge and share it with peers. Perhaps integrating information into a person's work flow should also include teaching it to others.

Best Practices for Encouraging a Self-Educating Mob

Mobs can be self-sufficient, but a healthy mob will need some encouragement to grow and thrive as a self-educating unit. Have some best practices in mind that can help you help the mob. There are things an organization can do to promote the growth and health of its mob. These practices mostly revolve around creating an atmosphere that is conducive to a mob that can care for themselves within an organizational structure. These are best practices for organizations that promote an atmosphere of openness, and not sub-version of the system. The system should work for the mob, not against it.

Other best practices included here address ways that individual members can help their mob to thrive. These practices encourage the mob through leadership, encouragement, and team building. A healthy mob needs leadership, and that leadership can come from anyone, perhaps even you.

An organization with a growing, vibrant mob will:

- Allow the mob to choose their own path. A healthy mob will have the power to choose what skills and knowledge they need to be better. The organization should encourage autonomy in the mob by avoiding mandates from above. The mob should be given power over decisions that affect them. The mob should also be allowed to review and choose the tools and technologies that best suit their needs. Mobs that choose their own tools may or may not—depending on their knowledge—need some technical guidance from IT members.

- View instructors as guideposts, not guides. Instructors and teachers are more mentors than coaches in a self-governed mob. Instructors will point the way, encourage, and be cheerleaders. They should not take over the direction of the mob. They should gently keep the mob from going too far astray, like a facilitator, but they do not need to draw the map. Instructors supply the pencils, paper, and compasses.

- Enable instructors to be more like advocates than traditional teachers. The instructors should be fans of their mobs, promoting their work and talking about them to everyone who will listen. An instructor who is an advocate, instead of a teacher, will enable the mob to find new ways to seek knowledge on their own without feeding skills to them directly.

- Create learning environments that promote interaction and participation, not passivity. A good mob will have people who contribute to the whole. In order for people to contribute, they must be given the tools and encouragement to do so. Organizations should choose learning environments that facilitate the ability to teach, share, create, and discuss. Environments that focus on a single teacher and many learners are not conducive to a self-educating mob. Likewise, environments with few capabilities, no flexibility, and walls do not promote, but often hinder, learning in meaningful ways.

- Create a transparent learning environment. Transparency will promote trust and loyalty in the mob for the parent organization and for the mob itself. An open environment will enable the mob to have honest discussion, discussions that involve synthesis and debate. Synthesis—combining multiple ideas to create a new concept—promotes learning and acquisition of knowledge.[2] Transparency is important to an environment in which people feel comfortable sharing and having real interactions.

- Understand that the success of a mob increases as the mob grows larger and more diverse. Diversity in its broadest sense in a mob adds a rainbow of ideas, experiences, and expertise. This diversity can help the mob overcome tendencies that can be destructive in group decisions.[3]

- Promote flexibility, experimentation, and learning from mistakes. The mob should be encouraged to try new things, experiment with instruction styles, and trial tools. The mob should be able to learn from failures and use the knowledge gained to be better next time. A flexible organization will be more concerned with the outcome than the process. Red tape should be reduced or completely removed. Procedures should not be used as a restraining method and guide for the mob. Few things have the power to deflate a mob and their individual members faster than inflexibility. Inflexibility implies distrust and a mob knows when they are not trusted. An organization that does not trust its mob will not have a healthy mob for long.

- Use both high- and low-tech options for learning environments and mob interactions. In order to reach the most learning styles, many different formats and facilitation styles should be offered. Allowing groups to choose their own formats and spaces for discussion will increase the probability that the mobs will choose methods that speak to them directly. An organization that fosters its mob will allow the mob the ability to choose these tools and methods for itself.

- Offer options for the mob to meet informally in physical spaces. Face-to-face interactions will promote discussion and a sense of identity and team within the mob. A sense of ownership and team identity will promote individual loyalty to the mob and the parent organization.

- Celebrate all successes, large and small. When your mob and its individuals shine, make sure that you are their biggest, most effusive fan.

A mob member who helps the crowd grow and learn will:

- Be willing to experiment with individuals' learning styles. You may know that you prefer to work at your own pace, test things, and learn from mistakes. You may not like working with large groups of people. You may prefer reflection and quiet learning. You may prefer chaos and artistic representations of concepts. Whatever expression your learning normally takes, try to be flexible. When a group is teaching each other, many different learning styles will be employed. This means that sometimes your preferred style will not be the one chosen. Try to adapt and be as flexible as possible. If something is presented in such a way that it is a barrier to learning, consider retooling the information in a style that fits you and then sharing it with the group. This will increase your own understanding of a concept as you teach it to others and your presentation may speak directly to someone else.

- Be flexible and transparent. Given the above example, retooling knowledge to meet different learning styles, individuals within the mob should be able to contribute in ways that are both easy and meaningful. Contributing should be something that is expected of all members. Methods of sharing should be transparent. This means that there are no gatekeepers to the process or the information. The mob is their own gatekeeper. Each individual will contribute to the transparency by discussing challenges and solutions openly. Conversations should happen in the open, with everyone who chooses to participate able to do so. Individuals who are uncomfortable with the fluidness of open conversations should strive for flexibility and a release of the belief that everything must be strictly ordered. However, every group needs a good facilitator and general organizer and perhaps this is the place on which your control efforts should be placed, with a gentle hand.

- Be willing to admit fear, lack of knowledge, or a general disagreement with the group. The practice of being transparent with your group about reservations, fears, or lack of knowledge essentially means that you should not allow these things to become an obstacle for the group. By admitting an issue with the group or the consensus of the group, you are participating as a transparent member. A discussion of the different sides of a process or information can be beneficial; it can help define the beliefs and increase the functionality of the mob. While constantly being a devil's advocate is not advisable, occasionally being a questioning force can be a good thing. Admitting a lack of knowledge will allow other members to flex their ability to teach other people, and this is essential to a self-educating mob. Differences of opinion should be seen as an opportunity to educate each other and to find common ground.

- Synthesize new information when presenting it to the group instead of listing facts. Recall is a lower-level learning skill than synthesis, which requires not only acquisition of a fact but an understanding of it. Mobs who engage in higher-level learning and discussion together will be more successful.[4] Synthesis discussions tend to be deeper and of better quality. Quality group discussions and sense-making are an excellent way to build the identity of a group because members will feel they have traveled a path together.

- Give context to the knowledge shared with the group. When teaching a skill or an idea, the context should always be given for the information shared. The context could be based on the individual's work experience or research, or be a background on the idea itself. Context can convey how an idea has evolved or how a skill was acquired. Giving context helps others understand the instructor and the idea being shared. Context leads to higher-level learning, synthesis, and sense-making, and fosters a sense of the mob's identity.[5]

- Be an encourager. This may be the most important thing in this list of practices, overshadowed only by the next two on the list. Every mob needs an encourager, and that encourager can be you. Make it your business to notice when someone does a good job and tell them, in front of the group, that you noticed. Notice when people step out of their comfort zones for the mob and acknowledge the effort publicly. Public praise can be powerful. Do keep in mind that you may have some personalities in the group that prefer private praise. If the group tries something and fails, be the first to ask what can be learned from the experience so that you can be better next time. Encourage the mob to teach each other. Be a cheerleader. Foster good will. Champion the mob's efforts. All successful mobs have someone encouraging them and acknowledging their work in some way. This does not mean that you are a "yes man." It means that you simply notice a good job and point it out to the mob. Being the encourager is a great, feel-good job whose importance should never be overlooked.

- Be the leader the mob needs. This is the most important thing for an individual of a mob to understand. Every group needs a leader, and that leader could be you. The most amazing thing about a mob is that the leadership can come from anywhere in the organization. Mobs that encourage leadership in unlikely places will find they have many talented facilitators on their hands. A mob with many leaders will be able to take on many projects at the same time. Leadership is something that you can choose to do. Seth Godin wrote an amazing book entitled *Tribes,* which calls all of us to find our tribe and lead it somewhere great. He says that "leadership is a choice. It's the choice to not do nothing."[6] A mob will need some direction. Choose to step up and suggest one. You may be the leader the mob needs to be outstanding.

- Celebrate all successes, large and small. When your mob or its individuals shine, make sure that you are their biggest, most effusive fan.

Education and knowledge sharing should be about the ideas, not about the talking head presenting them. Every practice and argument for a self-educating group or knowledge ecosystem comes down to a belief in the crowd's wisdom and the importance of the information the crowd holds.[7] Everyone has something of value to share. We all have passions. Every mob has the potential to do amazing, profession-altering, world-changing things. All mobs need is a place to grow and some proper care.

Endnotes

1. Don Tapscott and Anthony D. Williams, *Wikinomics: How Mass Collaboration Changes Everything* (New York: Portfolio, 2008), Kindle ebook: Location 532.

2. Francis Descantis, Anne-Laure Fayard, and Lu Jiang, "Learning in Online Forums," *European Management Journal* 21, no. 5 (October 2003): 565–577.

3. James Surowiecki, *The Wisdom of Crowds* (New York: Anchor, 2005), Kindle ebook: Location 601–603.

4. Francis Descantis, Anne-Laure Fayard, and Lu Jiang, "Learning in Online Forums."

5. Ann Majchrzak, Arvind Malhotra, and Richard John, "Perceived Individual Collaboration Know-How Development Through Information Technology–Enabled Contextualization: Evidence From Distributed Teams," *Information Systems Research* 16, no. 1 (March 2005): 9–27.

6. Seth Godin, *Tribes: We Need You to Lead Us* (New York: Portfolio, 2008): 59.

7. James Surowiecki, *The Wisdom of Crowds,* Kindle ebook: Location 2721–2722.

CHAPTER ELEVEN

Education Case Studies

These case studies were chosen because they represent either the best of their class, as with the LIS 768 example, or an innovation that has potential far beyond its original application, as with the examples of Five Weeks to a Social Library and the Learning 2.0 Program. They are all scalable for many different topics, programs, and uses, and were successful in nurturing their mobs because they created a knowledge ecosystem that was transparent, flexible, creative, and fun. All of these examples happen to come from libraries, librarians, or higher education. Companies outside of libraryland or education tend not to put similar programs on the open web; this may be because companies hide training modules on intranets or behind walls meant to keep outsiders like me away. It will be interesting indeed when some companies begin to be more open with their content and allow others to see the good knowledge ecosystems they have built.

Although the specific examples are in libraries or higher education, these case studies have elements that can be applied to different environments, organizations, and professions. In the future, I hope more companies choose to create open knowledge ecosystems for their members and then share those environments with the rest of the world via the internet. Learning occurs best when it is open and diverse, and we all have something important to share.

Dominican University LIS 768

Michael Stephens, assistant professor at Dominican University's Graduate School of Library and Information Science, teaches LIS 768: Library 2.0 & Social Networking Technologies (lis768.tamethe web.com).[1] This course is designed to immerse students in collaborative technology and educate graduate students about technology and community by using technology and community as learning tools. Stephens has moved away from traditional class portals like Blackboard and instead uses WordPressMU (WPMU), an open source, multiblogging tool as the learning management system (LMS). (For more information about the use of WPMU as an LMS in Stephens's LIS classes, see the interview with Kyle Jones in Chapter 8.)

Stephens and Jones use the BuddyPress plug-in with WPMU, which has a Facebook-like page layout. This allows flexibility with content, easy integration of outside information and media, and a central place to gather all the work being generated by the class into one fluid site. All of the content for the class, created by Stephens and the students, is gathered into one easy-to-navigate site. The class assignments, expectations, syllabus, student blogs, student groups, and discussion areas are given almost equal importance in terms of site real estate. Content generated by the students takes center stage. The richness of the learning environment is determined by the depth of what the students create during their journey through the class. The class does meet in person over three weekends in a face-to-face (f2f) setting, but all of the class content, from assignments to backchannel chatter, happens online. The blogs, and their content, are then aggregated into the main class site.

The bottom right of the home page for the LIS 768 site contains a display of current activity in Stephens's other two LIS classes. Figure 11.1 is a screenshot from the spring semester of 2010. Because each class site changes from semester to semester, the sites for the other classes may contain different elements and have a different layout.

Figure 11.1

LIS 768
The course site for Michael Stephens' 768 class

| Home | Activity | Community | Welcome to LIS768 | Weekend Schedules | Class Modules | Assignments | Tools |

reading buddy lists canada cell phones chat community
:ompetencies conference daily show david DDR design
ichotomy digital photo effect downers grow public library dreaming DVDs eBooks EBSCO email
tiquette film discussion group firefox flickr flock folksonomies formats fun
rture gadgets GAIM game google google maps google talk harry potter hoax HOWTO iChat
LO5 ILS IM security IM technique instant
messaging international iPod iTunes jabber jenny
essamyn librarian action figure librarian in black library journal library
uccess vale LIRT meebo metafilter metropolitan library system
michael MSN netherlands netlibrary mixtypen north suburban library
ystem NPR older librarians OPACs OPML over complicated p2p patriot act pencil
harpener pew internet planning pop culture powerbook PR
presentations printing privacy private sector

Welcome to LIS 768

Create an account, fill out your profile, get to know your fellow
students, and explore your class site.
Sign-up here »

Already a member?

| Username | .... | Log In | Sign Up |

☐ Remember Me

From the Class Blog

Take your blog with you!
Course Web Site Survey for Kyle & Michael
Mob Rule Learning Book: Request for Quotes
Hey Class! Help with Bulletin Blurb?
Weekend 3 Schedule Finalized

Groups   Newest | Active | Popular

Class Group
26 members

Personal Learning Networks
6 members

Serving Youth & Teens "Born Digital"
5 members

Looking for the Site Wide Activity?

Visit the Activity page for more...

Who's Online Avatars

There are no users currently online

Recently Active Member Avatars

Search

[   ]

| Members ▼ | Search |

🔲 **Blog Posts from LIS 701 & 753**

michael wrote a new blog post: Week 15: Labyrinth &
Course Wrap Up May 6, 2010

Martha wrote a new blog post: The Staffless Library
May 6, 2010

Cheryl Riendeau wrote a new blog post: Weekly Top
3 #2 May 5, 2010

kyle (tech support) wrote a new blog post: Take your
blog with you! May 1, 2010

kyle (tech support) wrote a new blog post: Take your
blog with you! May 1, 2010

This is the homepage for the spring 2010 LIS 768 class. Many elements are visible on the front page, and there are many pathways to reach the same information. This supports multiple learning pathways. (Screenshot taken from lis768.tametheweb.com by the author)

This page expands the course content beyond the class itself. In this way, the classes are encouraged to look outside of their own learning spaces. The simple fact that this class is not shut behind walls of a proprietary software, but is on the open web, means that the world is literally the classroom for the students and that the world can interact with them as they learn.

Using input from the students themselves, Stephens has changed the course title to Participatory Service & Emerging Technologies. Here is a portion of the course description in its current iteration:

The evolving web and related emerging technologies are signifiers of a broader cultural shift: toward an open, collaborative and participatory society. This course examines emerging technologies within a framework of participatory, "hyperlinked" library service: a model of creating, extending, updating and evaluating libraries via a user-centered approach.[2]

Requirements of the course are as follows:

Students will create blogs and get accounts at various social network sites. This is required for success in LIS 768. Students will also be expected to use the course website multiple times a week to stay up to date with readings, assignments, discussion and blogging. This is also a way for LIS 768 students to experience the emerging social nature of the web—similar systems are being used in library settings all over the world. Librarians are working, writing, and sharing in open, online systems created for interaction with each other and with library users. The LIS 768 site utilizes the WPMU software package to create an interactive environment for sharing and discourse. You must create an account on the site but no one in class is required to share their full name, photo, or any other details. The use of avatars and aliases is acceptable.

There are not true rules for this course, but there are guidelines: "Respect yourself. Respect each other. Respect the space."

LIS 768 is a technology-heavy course. Students are asked to use many different types of online tools. The degree to which each student is familiar with each tool varies, so Stephens has a set of online tutorials for each tool type used. In true collaborative fashion, much of the video and content of the tutorial pages comes from other learning sites around the web. Much of this material is freely available under a Creative Commons (CC) license. Creating a great class online is not about reinventing the wheel; it is about using other people's wheels as training wheels for your bike.

Participation online and in class makes up a quarter of each student's final grade, but there is no formula for how that participation is measured. Dr. Stephens expects his students to act like intelligent adults and take ownership of their learning experience. To truly experience the class and learn the material, the student has to actively participate in conversations and create new content for the class itself. Less-engaged students will not only be less present in conversations, but they will also fail to grasp the depth of the course content. This is no different than a traditional class in which students who skip sessions miss important material delivered by the instructor.

There are three different communication methods on the class site itself: through blogs and blog comments, in forums, and in groups. It appears that most of the class discussion occurred on the blogs, in posts and comments, and in the class's backchannels. In many courses, f2f or online, discussions in the class are centered on questions that the instructor poses. Because the discussions in LIS 768 centered on the blog posts, we know that the discussion was generated entirely by the students themselves. Stephens did give the students some topic areas on which they were to write reflections, but a topic area is very different from a leading question posed by a teacher. The students formulated their own ideas and questions about the topics and then discussed them with their fellow students, and the world, on their blogs. They determined their journey. Stephens was only there to provide signage along the way.

Backchannels, although not a part of the official class site, were cited frequently by the students in the discussions on the main class site. The term *backchannel* usually refers to any ongoing, real-time conversation that occurs simultaneously to a speech or presentation. In the end-of-class reflection posts, of which many are quoted later in this chapter, the backchannel was frequently described to have made individuals feel like they were part of a functional and cohesive team. That the backchannel was important—both to the creation of the class as a functional unit and to the students' learning process—is not something that should be dismissed. At a time when many students in higher education are at odds with their professors over the use of laptops in the classroom, the LIS students in Stephens's class are encouraged to chat online with each other. Many professors fight against technology in the classroom that they see as disruptive, but perhaps they have just not learned how to properly harness this powerful tool for the good of their classes.[3] It is also possible that these professors have not learned how to relate to and engage their students regarding the subject they teach. This is a more troubling issue, but beyond the scope of this book.

There were two different kinds of backchannels used for the Spring 2010 LIS 768 course. During f2f classes, the backchannel was a classwide Meebo chat room. This gave students another venue for topic exploration, and the chat room was occasionally so busy that some students commented on their blogs that they had to ignore the chatting because it was too much extra noise. The interesting thing to note here is that the students had a choice whether to tune in or not. When the class was not meeting f2f, there was a backchannel on Twitter, which was also quite lively. The hashtag for the class was *#LIS768*. On Twitter, discussions ranged from a support system for class problems, quips on class content, links to related information from around the web, and more mundane comments about food consumption.[4] What would the internet be without a good discussion of what we had for dinner?

One assignment that the students complete is a book review, but this is not the kind of book review that you may remember doing in school. The possible book list is a long list of topical books that Stephens actually created with the help of other professional librarians. He put the core list on his blog and then asked for comments, additions, and discussions.[5] For the actual report, students are to read the book and then choose to either write a 300-word reflection or to create a media presentation with audio, video, or both. Students post their reflections or presentations on their blogs so that other people can see their work and comment on it. This means that though each student does not read the entire list of books, all of which are phenomenal, the student does get a flavor of many of the books, their importance to the library profession, and the impact they made on the student. Students are then free to debate and discuss the books themselves and the content that their fellow students have created.

This collaborative and creative approach to education means that students are exposed not only to the knowledge of the professor but also to the collective wisdom of their peers. The mob is allowed to take possession of the content of the class; the depth and direction of the discussion and the overall value of the class is not determined by the professor. The vibrancy of the knowledge ecosystem lies almost entirely at the feet of the students themselves. Stephens is a true light on the path, but the students blaze the trail. Students, entrusted with this sort of power, often achieve things above and beyond what the instructor requires or even imagines because the students are inspired by the power and knowledge they are given to create something unexpected and beautiful.

The last assignment in LIS 768 is a course reflection and wrap-up post on the students' blogs. The posts are insightful and inspiring. Their reflections show that they moved beyond a class to a self-organized team. They became a mob with meaning and direction, together and individually. The voices of the students make a better argument for collaborative and creative education spaces than I could ever craft. Below are excerpts from some of their posts.

> And while I know it may sound a little corny, I found my fellow students to be one of my favorite parts of this class. By having individual blogs to read, Twitter to communicate, and face to face interaction to pull it all

together, I feel like I got to know and connected with this class [in] more intensive ways that many of my other classes at Dominican. –Abby[6]

I have to say this is probably the first class I will be genuinely sad to leave. This has definitely been my favorite class not only because of the massive amount of things I have learned but also because it was so much fun being able to keep up with the backchannel while in class. –Kelley[7]

I actually feel a little guilty right now—course reflections like this are supposed to offer constructive criticisms and suggest improvements for the future. But I don't have anything to say about this class that isn't overwhelmingly positive! This is the best class I've had in the GSLIS program. Period. I'm going to miss it, and all of you, and Prof. Stephens, for a long time to come.

EDIT—I guess I do have one suggestion—I think the class would be better served in a less formal setting, without the desks sitting between us, someplace we could gather more in-the-round ... but I don't know if the university has a space like that with the level of technology the class requires. –John[8]

I would also like to share that I had an interesting experience because the class content is open and not on Blackboard. Right after my group's presentation got posted, the daughter of my library's Assistant Director sent her the link to our presentation! That was pretty neat. She must have an alert set up. This was a reminder that whatever goes up can be found. –Kim[9]

I think my favorite part of the class was the backchannel. Although I was completely unfamiliar with the concept at the beginning of the class, I got sucked in very quickly. I'd had a Twitter account for a while, but I'd only ever tweeted a few times. Now I'm tweeting several times a day ... Normally with this sort of weekend class it's hard to get to know people, but I feel like I've really gotten to know the people who have been active on Twitter ... I also really liked Michael's teaching style. It seems like a lot of professors are far more concerned with whether you rigidly follow their syllabus than whether you're learning anything. It was clear to me on the very first day that that was not the case in this class. I liked the flexibility we had to explore and discover the aspects of Library 2.0 that most interested us ... I think this was my biggest AHA! Moment—that the learning was the most important thing. Too often it seems like I'm only learning the material so I can get a good grade and the learning is just a means to an end. I learned more in this class than I do in most classes, and I think that's due in large part to the fact that I could explore what interested me— and almost all of it interested me! In many ways, Michael was more of a facilitator than a teacher, letting us guide the discussion and the topics we covered. I wish more profs could be like that. –Stacy[10]

The hybrid course offered the advantage to get to know Michael and my classmates both in person and in an online setting. Communicating, learning, and reading via Twitter was both fun and interesting, especially to view all the backchannel during class! –Heather[11]

This has been one of the most insightful classes that I have ever taken in my graduate and undergraduate career. The subject matter was extremely interesting and I felt more engaged and connected doing the weekly assignments, than I have felt in most of my other classes. –Brianna[12]

After signing up, I was skeptical of the format of the course at first as I had never done an online or hybrid class. Despite our mostly online studies, I did really feel connected to my classmates. Following everyone on Twitter was definitely a unifying force. Also I thought that, surely, meeting for 17 hours over the course of a weekend would be *awful*. But it never was. I loved those days and found them passing almost too quickly. One of the first days, someone uttered the phrase "Library Camp," and my brain really took hold of that. I loved camp as a kid, and I know that now I'll miss these, my adult days of sitting clustered with friends learning new things and telling stories. –Elizabeth[13] (emphasis in the original)

Our class dynamic was also supportive of each others' ideas too. I wish I could have our class backchannel playing through all of my classes at Dominican! –Liz[14]

We all created our own niche online, and with the use of the backchannel (which I miss greatly), we were able to stay engaged with what was happening in the classroom. With the style of the assignments, reporting on the context books, and the group work, I feel like we were trusted intellectually and respected for the content we created. –Katy[15]

Taking the Conversation Online

It may not be feasible to construct your own LMS, as Kyle Jones and Michael Stephens did, but adding just one tool can change the dynamics of a mob that is learning together. Twitter has been successfully used in a handful of university classrooms for this purpose. The addition of this single easy-to-use tool completely changed the conversation in these classes and can change your group of students into a mob that learns, creates, and is a community.

Disruptive Technologies in Teaching and Learning

Cole W. Camplese and Scott McDonald co-teach the Disruptive Technologies in Teaching and Learning (www.blogs.tlt.psu.edu/courses/disruptive) graduate course at Pennsylvania State University. They use a combination of Twitter, Google Docs, and the Penn State blogs in their class, which does meet f2f weekly. Students are required to contribute to class discussions on Twitter, but there is no specific number of tweets they must reach. Instead, 100 points of "general participation" forms part of their overall grade. General participation is defined as "contributions to blog posts, comments in class, tweets, Delicious bookmarks added, and more."[16] Students are not required to use any one tool, but are instead encouraged to experiment and utilize many different forms of communication with their classmates.

An interesting teaching method emerged during the course of the class. As in Stephens's class, Twitter helped develop a sense of community between the students and instructors, both in and out of class, but that's not what really made a difference for the Disruptive Technologies in Teaching and Learning class. Camplese said that Twitter became "essential" and was "the most powerful backchannel I have been a part of in a learning environment."[17] During class, Camplese and McDonald projected two screens onto the wall, one with their slides for the lecture, and one showing the live stream of Twitter comments. Students would ask questions of their instructors and each other, but more importantly, they used Twitter to post additional resources during the class discussion. Twitter gave the f2f class meetings immediacy and allowed students to discuss topics in real time.

U.S. History II

Monica Rankin also used Twitter in her U.S. History II course at the University of Texas at Dallas. This class met three times a week, had 90 students enrolled, and was taught in an auditorium-style room. Rankin decided to use Twitter because she "wanted to find a way to incorporate more student-centered learning techniques and involve the students more fully into the material."[18] In a class of 90, a normal class discussion does not work well, but Rankin wanted students to be able to discuss the material. She chose Twitter because, although many students did not have laptops, almost all of them had cell phones with text messaging, which Twitter supports. Rankin used a different hashtag for each week's class, so that the discussions were searchable by week and reading topic.

Instead of using Twitter as a backchannel, as other classes have done, Rankin's class used Twitter on Fridays, when there was no lecture. The class had reading assignments to be completed by Friday and when they came to class, they used Twitter to discuss the readings. This type of interaction gave the 90-person class an intimate way to have class discussions and leveled the field with so many students needing to participate. Unlike with other examples used in this book, discussions between the students outside of class were rare. So, although Twitter promoted unity during the class, it did not foster a community outside of it. One problem that Rankin did notice was that the first 2 weeks of discussion had to be spent helping students set up accounts and figure out the tool. Though they were asked to do this outside of class, students did not complete that task on their own. Rankin also found that the discussions were better when she walked the room, answering questions and assisting students.

From Memex to YouTube

Gardner Campbell teaches FYS 1399 From Memex to YouTube: Introduction to New Media Studies at Baylor University in Waco, Texas (www.gardnercampbell.wetpaint.com/page/FYS+1399+Memex +to+YouTube+F09).[19] In this class, Campbell used Twitter as a backchannel for the f2f lecture classes. Students accessed Twitter via their own laptops during class. This example is unique, because in addition to the students and Campbell, there was also a librarian participating in the class Twitter discussions. Ellen Hampton Filgo is the elearning librarian at Baylor University, and she logged on to Twitter at the beginning of each session and was greeted by the students. During the class, Filgo commented on the discussion, answered student questions, and pointed them to resources that could be found online or in the library. Often, students would ask about things related to the class content that were not part of the main discussion. In one instance, for example, a student asked whether there were archives for a particular author. Filgo was happy to tell him that there were three libraries that held archives for that author.[20]

This group saw additional benefits outside of the classroom. Students often continued their discussions when classes were over, and Filgo said that students sought her out, both online and in person, for research help with this and other classes. One student said in a survey at the end of the semester, "I, prior to Dr. Campbell's class and Ms. Filgo's participation in the class, was not aware of the vast amount of resources the library had such as chat, online resources, and the librarians themselves."[21] Students had access to research help from the beginning of their research process.

These three examples of Twitter use in an academic classroom show three different ways to capitalize on fostering communication and community in a learning environment. Twitter was a tool that created a powerful backchannel in a class that already had good f2f discussion. In Camplese and McDonald's class, Twitter created a real-time discussion that allowed for a wider topic field and created a community for the class outside of the classroom. For Monica Rankin, Twitter allowed her to incorporate discussions into a class that otherwise would have been too large to handle any discussions at all, and students could use texting when a laptop was not available. Campbell's students were able to share resources, create community, and get real-time research help from a librarian. These tools individually are wonderful, but if a single class could do all of this collectively, it would be amazing.

Five Weeks to a Social Library

Five Weeks to a Social Library (www.sociallibraries.com/course) was a project I was involved in during the spring of 2006. This was a free, grassroots, online course that was created by librarians, for librarians. We created it for two reasons: We saw a need for librarians to have access to continuing education about technology practices in libraries and we were told we could not create a quality class for free, using free tools. I learned that you should never tell a motivated mob of individuals that they "can't" do something. What they hear is actually, "Go do something unique and wonderful to prove me wrong."

Like the LIS 768 class discussed earlier in this chapter, we used the tools to teach the tools. We chose 40 participants from all over the world to go through the class. We had more than 100 applicants, but we felt that as a first endeavor, we wanted the groups to be small. We wanted to be able to interact with the students and to have the students interact with each other. There were weekly readings, chats, webcasts, and many opportunities to interact and learn. Every participant was placed into a weekly chat group that was moderated by one of the six creators of the course. Everything created for the course was licensed under a CC Attribution Non-Commercial Share Alike license. This meant that all the course content is available to others as long as they link back to Five Weeks. Our use of the CC license enabled other instructors to use our content in their own online learning environments.

Each week had a different technology theme and we asked other librarians who were working with those tools to create webcasts and then appear as guests in chats on that topic area. Librarians who created content for the program donated their time for free. Our intention was that the unique content created for the class could be reused by libraries and librarians for their own training, in groups or individually. Webcasts were live, but then archived for people who could not make the time slot that week. The live webcasts had a chat that ran simultaneously so that presenters and participants could interact during the presentations. Amazingly, the content is still being used and the model is one that the profession has repeated in many different forms.

Participants were asked to write weekly reflections on the topics, which ranged from blogs and social networking to overcoming resistance to technology. For the final project, participants were asked to draft a proposal for their library on the use of a tool discussed in the class. The form of the proposal—paper, memo, or a mockup of the tool itself—was the individual's choice. All of the participants were practicing librarians, so we wanted them to be able to take their proposals to their libraries and present them to their boards, directors, or peers if they chose to do so. Each group gave feedback to fellow group members on how to improve their projects, and many of them used their proposal to successfully introduce new tools and programs to their staff. We still occasionally get feedback and comments on this project. The level of participation in Five Weeks, which the students did on their own time for no credit, was amazing.

Five Weeks to a Social Library is a perfect example of a self-educating mob. A group of librarians recognized a gap in the continuing education opportunities and decided to create the learning environment needed for their peers. We enlisted the help of other librarians that were already doing great things in their libraries with social software. None of the six organizers would have been able to create something like this on her own at the time. Even with six of us wrangling the 40 participants, we still looked outside our circle for experts on particular tools to do the weekly webcasts. Experts donated their time gladly, because they all believed that continuing education and knowledge sharing were and are important to the growth of our profession.

Five Weeks to a Social Library was important because it was free, it was created with free tools, it involved librarians from many different kinds of libraries, and it was not associated with a governing organization. This was a true grassroots effort. It is a model that can be used in an endless number of different applications in almost any industry. The topic of this course was social software in libraries, but it could have easily been marketing, customer relations, or team management.

Learning 2.0 Project

The Learning 2.0 Project (www.plcmclearning.blogspot.com) at the public library of Charlotte & Mecklenburg County in Charlotte, North Carolina, was designed in 2006 by librarian Helene Blowers. She was inspired by the 43 Things (www.43things.com) website and an article by Stephen Abram in which he challenged the reader to learn 43 new technology tools and skills.[22] Blowers created a learning program for her library in which staff members were encouraged to learn 23 new technologies over the course of 9 weeks. (Blowers reduced the number of tasks from 43 to 23 to better fit her 9-week timeline.) Figure 11.2 is a screenshot of some of the 23 tasks staff were asked to complete.

Staff members were not required to complete the program, but they were offered some great incentives to do so. Staff members who finished the program by an early date were entered into a drawing for

Figure 11.2

---

23 Learning 2.0 Things*

(Note: Details about each task will be activated every week with posts related to each item)

Week 1: Introduction (official start of week August 7th)
1. Read this blog & find out about the program.
2. Discover a few pointers from lifelong learners and learn how to nurture your own learning process.

Week 2: Blogging
3. Set up your own blog & add your first post.
4. Register your blog on PLCMC Central and begin your Learning 2.0 journey.

Week 3: Photos & Images
5. Explore Flickr and learn about this popular image hosting site.
6. Have some Flickr fun and discover some Flickr mashups & 3rd party sites.
7. Create a blog post about anything technology related that interests you this week.

Week 4: RSS & Newsreaders
8. Learn about RSS feeds and setup your own Bloglines newsreader account.
9. Locate a few useful library related blogs and/or news feeds.

Week 5: Play Week
10. Play around with an online image generator.
11. Take a look at LibraryThing and catalog some of your favorite books.
12. Roll your own search tool with Rollyo.

Week 6: Tagging, Folksonomies & Technorati
13. Learn about tagging and discover a Del.icio.us (a social bookmaking site)
14. Explore Technorati and learn how tags work with blog posts.
15. Read a few perspectives on Web 2.0, Library 2.0 and the future of libraries and blog your thoughts.

Week 7: Wikis
16. Learn about wikis and discover some innovative ways that libraries are using them.
17. Add an entry to the Learning 2.0 SandBox wiki.

Week 8: Online Applications & Tools
18. Take a look at some online productivity (word processing, spreadsheet) tools.

This is part of the original list of 23 Things. Many of the links lead to a short tutorial podcast. (Screenshot taken from www.plcmcl2-things.blogspot.com by the author) a PDA, and participants who completed the program by a later date were entered into a drawing for a new laptop. Everyone who completed the program received a USB MP3 player. In 3 short months, 362 staff members started the program and 222 completed it by one of the deadlines. For an activity that was not required, the level of participation shows what a few small incentives can do for a program.

Over the 9 weeks, staff were asked to do two to three tasks per week. Each week included a short podcast introducing the tool of the week or showing how the tool could be used. The other one or two tasks were usually exploration of the tool and a reflection post. Each participant in the program created his or her own blog on Blogger (www.blogger.com) to record the progress through the program. Each item on the list was a short learning task, something that a staff member could do in a handful of minutes during a busy work day.

The Learning 2.0 method has been adapted by hundreds of libraries, teachers, and schools. Learning 2.0 was featured in *Wired* magazine and a *New York Times* podcast.[23] It is a system that works well because it can be done in small chunks; it encourages self-discovery, creation, and sharing; and it offers incentives that are meaningful to the participants. All of the content created for the original 23 Things Learning 2.0 Project is licensed under CC to share and use, and Blowers started a new blog, Learning 2.1 (www.explorediscoverplay.blogspot.com), to create an ongoing list of new things people can explore to keep their technology skills fresh.

Endnotes

1. Since this case study was conducted, Dr. Stephens has left Dominican University and is currently an assistant professor at San Jose State University's (SJSU) School of Library and Information Science. At the time of this publication, LIS 768 at Dominican University is no longer being offered; Dr. Stephens is teaching LIBR 287 Seminar in Information Science at SJSU, which covers current issues and problems in information science. Dr. Stephens continues to employ integration of social media and student centered teaching in his courses.

2. Michael Stephens, "Hey Class! Help With Bulletin Blurb?" LIS 768, lis768.tametheweb.com/blog/2010/04/14/hey-class-help-with-bulletin-blurb/ (accessed July 19, 2011).

3. Tovia Smith, "Put Away That Laptop: Professors Pull the Plug," *NPR, Weekend Edition Saturday* (April 24, 2010), www.npr.org/templates/story/story.php?storyId=126241853 (accessed July 19, 2011).

4. Twitter, #LIS768, www.twitter.com/#search?q=%23lis768 (accessed July 19, 2011).

5. Michael Stephens, "LIS 768 Reading List," Tame the Web (September 10, 2008), tametheweb.com/2008/09/10/lis768-reading-list (accessed July 19, 2011).

6. Abby, "Class Finale Post," Library 2.0 Escapades, community.tametheweb.com/abbyn/2010/04/21/class-finale-post (accessed July 19, 2011).

7. Kelley Plass, "Course Wrap-up," Fedlibdreamer, lis768.tametheweb.com/kelleyblog/2010/04/22/course-wrap-up (accessed July 19, 2011).

8. John Keogh, "Course Reflection & Wrap Up," Lost in the Tubes, community.tametheweb.com/lostinthetubes (accessed July 19, 2011).

9. Kim Crawshaw, "Course Wrap Up," Kim 2.0, community.tametheweb.com/continuedexploration/2010/04/23/course-wrap-up (accessed July 19, 2011).

10. Stacy Taylor, "Course Reflection," Stacy, community.tametheweb.com/glowing fish/2010/04/23/course-reflection (accessed July 19, 2011).

11. Heather Ontko, "Course Reflection," Heather's Blog: LIS 768, lis768.tametheweb.com/heathero/2010/04/24/course-reflection (accessed July 19, 2011).

12. Brianna, "Class Reflection," Breezy in the City, community.tametheweb.com/bandersonlis768/2010/04/25/class-reflection (accessed July 19, 2011).

13. Elizabeth Ludemann, "2.0 Reflections," Ludeeliz, lis768.tametheweb.com/ludeeliz/2010/04/25/2-0-reflections (accessed July 19, 2011). Note: The author of this post did not permanently archive her profile and content so the original link is no longer active.

14. Liz Novak, "Warning! Cheesy Class Reflection Alert!" Library Lasso, 2010, lis768.tametheweb.com/librarylasso/2010/04/25/warning-cheesey-class-reflection-alert (accessed July 19, 2011).

15. Katy Hite, "Well, That's a Wrap," The Webrairan for Your Bohemia, community. tametheweb.com/bohemianwebrarian (accessed July 19, 2011).

16. Cole Camplese and Scott McDonald, "Spring 2010 Syllabus Disruptive Technologies in Teaching and Learning," Penn State Blogs, blogs.tlt.psu.edu/courses/disruptive/2009/10/spring-2010-syllabus.html (accessed July 19, 2011).

17. Cole Camplese, "Connections," I Like the Internets ... A Lot, colecamplese. typepad.com/my_blog/2008/05/connections.html (accessed July 19, 2011).

18. Monica Rankin, *Some General Comments on the Twitter Experiment*, www.ut dallas.edu/~mar046000/usweb/twitterconclusions.htm (accessed July 19, 2011).

19. Since this case study was conducted, Dr. Campbell has left Baylor University and is currently the director of Professional Development and Innovative Initiatives in the Learning Technologies Department and is an associate professor of English in the department of Literature, Language, and Culture at Virginia Tech. At the time of publication, Baylor is not currently offering FYS 1399 From Memex to YouTube. Dr. Campbell continues to be an advocate for social media in the classroom through his work with other educators, his teaching, and writing.

20. Ellen Hampton Filgo, "A Librarian and a Hashtag: Embedded Virtually in a Classroom Via Twitter," conference presentation at LOEX 2010, docs.google.com/present/view?id=ddzmkrn5_345gtjgjccw&revision=_latest&start=0&theme=blank&cwj=true (accessed July 19, 2011).

21. Part of an interview with Ellen Hampton Filgo conducted over Google Docs.

22. Stephen Abram, "43 Things I Might Want to Do This Year," *Information Outlook*, findarticles.com/p/articles/mi_m0FWE/is_2_10/ai_n16133338 (accessed July 19, 2011).

23. Helene Blowers, "Learning 2.0 in the News," Learning 2.0, plcmcl2-about.blogspot.com/2006/08/about-learning-20-project.html#contact (accessed July 19, 2011).

CHAPTER TWELVE

The Future of the Self-Educated Mob

It is unlikely that the pace of change will slow in the coming years; history has shown us that technology will continue to advance—and advance quickly. New services will be developed, new tools will change the way we do business, learn, and live, and there will be new processes to learn and examine. We will always strive to improve what we do. All of this means that the need for continuing education will grow, not diminish, over time. Training within organizations will be an ever-increasing, crucial, tangible need, which will have to be fulfilled. For many professions, especially ones related to technology and information, this need has already come to the forefront. The ways in which organizations handle this need separates good organizations from the dross.

Good organizations have taken steps to ensure that flexible training is part of the standard procedures and expectations within the organization. The two keys to success for these organizations are that they have a training mechanism in place and that the mechanism is flexible. The pace and growth of technology demands that we as individuals and organizations be flexible. Training that is more focused on content, and not the talking head delivering the content, is inherently flexible because it does not hinge on one person.

Systems that do not rely on one tool alone will likewise be more flexible, as members can choose what fits their needs most at that time. A system that is nimble and quick from the beginning, one that adjusts to each learner and need, will succeed. Organizations that rely on a single talking head or are inflexible by nature will have a harder time adjusting than their more nimble counterparts. Technology tools emerge too quickly and often for organizations to lock themselves into a single tool. A knowledge ecosystem that includes a self-educating mob with many tools at its disposal is a system with infinite potential for growth and success.

That is not to say that continuing education programs within organizations should not have some supervision. Whether this supervision is provided by an individual or committee that steps in to facilitate when needed will depend on the organization. As discussed previously, even a well-reasoned and intelligent mob needs some direction at times from a "benevolent" leader.[1] Leaders who rise organically within the mob may be better than an appointed overseer. A director chosen by the mob will give the mob more of a sense of ownership. If the leader who rises has not previously been in a leadership position, this can be a growing opportunity for both the individual and the organization. Growing organizations will seek out and encourage this new leadership. Organizations with vibrant mobs will encourage the emergence and development of this leadership.

A fast-moving knowledge economy means that the education system will have to keep up. Using the knowledge of the mob increases the likelihood of training that keeps up with the changing landscape. The pace of change means that it's unrealistic to ask one or two trainers to keep up with everything, and then ask them to train others. Relying on the large and diverse pool of intelligence held by a mob is more likely to yield a mob that is well-trained and up-to-date with the latest developments. A single person would suffer from information overload trying to keep up with every new development in his or her field, while a mob has many eyes with which to choose the best of the latest developments to share. The mob requires only a knowledge ecosystem in which to plant their findings.

Practically, this means that a paradigm shift is in motion. The mob, previously students who were receptacles of someone else's knowledge, can now become both the learner and the instructor. If we, as students of any age, can mentor others while they in turn mentor us, we have created a self-sustaining knowledge ecosystem that can continue to grow as time passes, membership fluctuates, and organizational changes occur. Ecosystems are flexible with the seasons and change as new species are introduced; our learning systems should be as well. Knowledge ecosystems should not crumble when a single person leaves. Mobs should be able to adapt and continue with their primary objective, learning and sharing knowledge, intact and flourishing despite changes.

In university classrooms, this may mean that students take more control over the learning process. The instructor may guide the direction, but the mob will learn primarily through reflection and shared exploration within the group. This sort of learning environment does lend itself more to the humanities and social sciences. Though my understanding of the sciences is as rudimentary as any English major's, I think that this method of learning is harder to apply to science areas, though not impossible. Many of the most innovative projects today, like the Human Genome Project discussed in Chapter 9, are created by a cooperative mob—learning and sharing discoveries as they are made. There is no reason why other science-related fields and classrooms cannot follow suit.

The technology being used in the classrooms of higher education must adapt as well or these institutions will lose the ability to reach their students effectively. Students attending school now expect a level of integration between their lives, technology, and education. This expectation will increase over time because technology use will only increase. Technology integration and the expectations of students will set up a supply and demand relationship in which organizations that are more successful with technology will be more successful overall. More universities will step away from monolithic structures like Blackboard and integrate tools that are more flexible and open to different learning environments. This move will come in small steps, as professors turn to other methods of creating class portals or simply add new tools to the standard systems. This means letting go of the idea that all technology must integrate with the silo technology systems currently being used on campuses. It means that campus IT will have to release some control to their users in order to become more flexible. Universities will have to do a better job of supporting and training their instructors for the use and integration of technology. Staff members who provide support for instructional technology, like IT groups and librarians, will become even more important as instructors look for advocates, trainers, and advice.

In the workplace and professional organizations, a flexible knowledge ecosystem will be revolutionary for the groups that put faith and time into their mob. Organizations that provide the space and support to mobs to cultivate their own ecosystems will be vibrant organizations. Vibrancy breeds hope in individual members and loyalty to the group. A vibrant organization is alive and growing. Gone will be the dry learning workshops and the mind-numbing seminars. Organizations with members who are stuck on an unchanging track will find themselves stuck in a cul-de-sac as well. Staff training can be fun and relevant. Simply ask the mob members what they need to learn most or what skill they think will improve their job performance, and then ask them how they would like to solve this need.

Future mobs may not be connected to an organization at all. They may simply be a disparate group of people that has come together to learn something or form a support group. The ability of the internet to foster these kinds of relationships is perhaps the most exciting of all because there really are no limits to the growth of this kind of mob. A mob that is not constrained by an organization is responsible only to themselves. Its members will truly be the creators of their own destiny. These mob-created knowledge ecosystems, free of tethers from organizations, will be able to reach individuals anywhere. Organizations that utilize these groups will give their members access to learning opportunities with little to no effort on the part of the organization itself. Everyone benefits from this partnership.

Organizations and the halls of higher education can create and nurture a knowledge ecosystem with little effort and a whole lot of trust. Simply giving a mob a place to run free and then peeking into the pasture occasionally is all that most crowds require. It is such a small thing, to give space and transparency, but a small thing that has the potential to yield bountiful results.

Endnote

1. Jeff Howe, *Crowdsourcing: Why the Power of the Crowd Is Driving the Future of Business* (New York: Crown Business, 2008): 284.

A Conclusion and Manifesto

Every field will always have its experts and talking heads who will always be deferred to for many things. This will not change. However, we may come to realize that our crowds, our mobs of amateurs, can be just as effective in problem solving and in training as the handful of experts we have always relied on. We can keep the talking heads around for the occasional keynote or guest seminar, but the mob should also stretch their abilities.

Mobs have the collective knowledge and power to do anything, to be anything, to teach anything, to learn anything, and to solve anything. We cannot ignore this power forever. The force of it can change the world, if we set it free.

Many mobs simply need a place to grow and a single leader or two to blaze the trail. Take a chance and be a leader. Step up and offer your fellows your knowledge—and encourage them to share theirs as well. As a member of an organization, step out of your mold and do something new. Be a leader in your organization by not leading at all—allow your mob to do the leading for you. Give your mob a place to roam free, to play, to grow, and to impact your profession or your community.

Successful mobs are started because an individual or a small group decides it wants to do something different or be something better. Countries are formed this way. Problems are solved this way.

Organizations are made better this way. New communities are planted this way. Decide to do something different and be better.

Share what you know and help others to lead. Believe in the power of mob rule.

Tools and Glossary

The mob, in an effort to teach themselves and share their knowledge, has designed and refined many low-cost or free online tools. These tools are amazingly elegant in their scope, depth, and ability; they cover almost every need and can be applied to many different situations. All an individual or an organization needs is time to choose the right tool and a basic knowledge of how online tools function. You can find rows and rows of books and websites on choosing tools and the minutiae of using different tools over others. This appendix contains a general explanation of technology terms and definitions of tool types, including an explanation of the best use of each type, specific examples of popular tools, and other choices associated with choosing tools for your mob. Both the beginner and intermediate user will find these explanations helpful. The book's website at www.wanderingeyre.com/mobrule will have the newest examples of tools, as well as a plethora of other links to mob rule education-related resources.

What Does Free Really Mean?

What does free or low cost really mean? There is a saying in technology spheres that some tools are free, as in beer, but most are free, as in kittens. This is usually bandied about during discussions of open source software (OSS), which is introduced later in this appendix. Free beer is free. There is no overhead to free beer. The only long-standing repercussions of free beer are a friend gained and a pleasant buzz. Free kittens are not free. You may acquire the kitten for free, but a kitten has a high overhead cost. Kittens need food, trips to the veterinarian, and attention. Most free tools are free as in kittens, requiring some kind of upkeep or attention. When choosing tools, the amount of care and feeding the tool requires should be taken into consideration. Some tools will require quite a bit of knowledge and time, and some require minimal effort.

Tools That Live on Your Server

There are two main kinds of tools available online: tools that live on someone else's server and tools that live on your server. When talking about tools you host on your server, this means that you download the tool onto your own server and run it within or on your own system. Besides the obvious geographical issue of where the tool lives, the major differences between these types of tools are the level of IT support you need in order to maintain, customize, and control them. Many tool types, like blogs, wikis, and project management systems, have hosted and unhosted options or brands. Some specific tools will give you an option to download and install or to simply create an account (host it on someone else's server), but many only provide one option or the other.

The benefits of running a tool on your own server include:

- Customization: You are only constrained in its use by the ability level of the IT people you have working on it (unless the tool is proprietary; see a later discussion in the Appendix regarding proprietary tools).

- Branding: When you have more control over the tool, you are more likely to be able to brand the tool or make aesthetic changes.

- Security: You have more control over the security settings and can run the tool on your intranet or on the general internet, depending on your needs.

- Advertisements: Running a tool on your own server means that your version will not have unwanted advertisements (which many of the free, hosted versions of tools feature).

The challenges of running a tool on your own server include:

- Technical knowledge: Some rudimentary skills to install and maintain are required.

- Maintenance: General maintenance and upgrades can often become the biggest issue, especially for smaller organizations with little or no IT support or without a server of their own.

- Domain: You may need to acquire a domain for your tool depending on the use of the tool.

Open Source Software vs. Proprietary Tools

When you choose to host your own tool, you will have to make a decision about whether to use OSS or a proprietary tool. OSS is a tool with a source code open to developers and users. This means that production of OSS is completed and added onto by a large community of programmers and users. OSSs are created by the mob, for the mob.

The benefits of using OSS include:

- Communities of users and programmers can often answer questions and help troubleshoot problems with the tool.

- Open code is open-ended because the source code for the tool is available; with the right knowledge or skills you can customize the tool to do almost anything.

The challenges of using OSS include:

- Cost: Free as in kittens, not free as in beer. Some OSS communities will require a minimal fee for use and that fee usually goes toward technical support.

- Programming expertise: Needed in some cases, but not all. Some programming knowledge is needed to run and maintain the program. There are notable exceptions to this, including some blog and wiki tools.

- Documentation: Occasional complaints with some tools are that their code is not properly documented. This is important when customizing or troubleshooting a tool on your own.

The benefits of using a proprietary tool include:

- Technical support: You pay more money, but you also get customer service from a company.

- Programming expertise: Often you will need very little programming expertise to run a proprietary tool, especially if you are going to run it "out of the box," which means that you are going to run the tool exactly as it comes. For organizations with little or no IT support, this is often the reason why they choose proprietary over OSS.

The challenges of using a proprietary tool include:

- Cost: Proprietary software can cost a lot of money, especially if the cost is scaled per users or the size of your institution.

- Licensing: You do not own the tool, you license it, so you may be limited as to how you can use it.

- Closed code: Unlike OSS, the code for the tool is closed, so the customization and flexibility of the tool will be limited.

Tools That Are Hosted Elsewhere

Tools that are hosted elsewhere, or tools for which you create accounts online, live on someone else's server. For many people, this is the kind of tool that they encounter most often. Hosted tools will usually be limited in the customization that you can do in terms of aesthetics, branding, security, and features, but you will rarely need IT support for a hosted tool. Cost can vary widely, though with free tools you will often see advertisements. *Cloud computing*, a term coined in the last few years, is the idea that everything you do on your desktop can occur online, in the cloud, with tools that live on someone else's server.

Tool Types, Examples, and Best Use Practices

For a more complete and up-to-date list of tools, examples, readings, and best practices, please see the website for this book at www.wanderingeyre.com/mobrule.

Blogs

News, updates, learning journals, creating websites with a combination of frequent updates and static pages, multiple-authored websites, one-to-many or handful-to-many publishing:

- Blogger, www.blogger.com

- BuddyPress, www.buddypress.org

- Movable Type, www.movabletype.com or www.movabletype.org

- Six Apart TypePad, www.sixapart.com

- Squarespace, www.squarespace.com

- WordPress, www.wordpress.org or www.wordpress.com

Wikis

Training portals, data collaboration and gathering websites, many-to-many, democratic conversation and creation systems:

- MediaWiki, www.mediawiki.org

- PBworks, www.pbworks.com

- PmWiki, www.pmwiki.org

- WikiMatrix, www.wikimatrix.org (compares different wiki platforms)

Photos

Posting, sharing, and editing photos, widgets for using content in other media, and some integrate Creative Commons licensing:

- Flickr, www.flickr.com

- Photobucket, www.photobucket.com

- Picasa, www.picasa.google.com

- Picnik, www.picnik.com

- Showzey, www.showzey.com

Tagging

Creating a lexicon, gathering or storing URLs (multiple formats) by category or format type, using tags and RSS to create subject-specific lists, sharing resources among contacts or with RSS; many tools have tags built in to their platforms:

- Delicious, www.delicious.com

- Diigo, www.diigo.com

- Pinboard, pinboard.in

Podcasting

Pushing any type of audio content like reviews, talk (radio) shows, music, interviews:

- Audacity, www.audacity.sourceforge.net

RSS Creators/Syndication Tools

Gathers disparate feeds from multiple social media sites and puts them into one handy RSS feed for your faithful followers:

- Feedburner, feedburner.google.com

- FriendFeed, www.friendfeed.com

- Tumblr, www.tumblr.com

Videos and Presentations

Video sharing or traditional slide sharing from presentations, or a different kind of presentation:

- 280 Slides, www.280slides.com

- Animoto, www.animoto.com

- Prezi, www.prezi.com

- SlideShare, www.slideshare.net

- Ustream, www.ustream.tv

- YouTube, www.youtube.com

Live Blogging

Pulling information from multiple sites, like blogging, pictures, and Twitter, in real time during an event:

- CoveritLive, www.coveritlive.com

- ScribbleLive, www.scribblelive.com

- WordPress Live Blogging plug-in, www.wordpress.org/extend/plugins/live-blogging

Survey Tools

Online surveys and data gathering:

- Polldaddy, www.polldaddy.com

- SurveyGizmo, www.surveygizmo.com

- SurveyMonkey, www.surveymonkey.com

- Zoomerang, www.zoomerang.com

Content Management Systems

OSSs that allow multiple users to be content creators of a website; very flexible and can used for almost anything, including creating learning environments:

- Drupal, www.drupal.org

- Joomla!, www.joomla.org

- LightCMS, www.speaklight.com

- Pligg, www.pligg.com

- WordPress, www.wordpress.org

Course Management Systems or Learning Management Systems

Builds a learning environment that manages the learning process from discovery to discussion to grading:

- Blackboard, www.blackboard.com

- HotChalk, www.hotchalk.com

- Moodle, www.moodle.org

- Sakai, www.sakaiproject.org

- WordPress, www.wordpress.org

Group Management Systems and Social Networks

Creates groups for events, meetings, organizations, to complete tasks or just for fun:

- Basecamp, www.basecamphq.com

- Facebook, www.facebook.com

- Google Groups, www.groups.google.com

- Meetup, www.meetup.com

- Yahoo! Groups, www.groups.yahoo.com

- Ning, www.ning.com

Collaboration Tools

Collaborate, create, and share:

- Google Docs, www.docs.google.com

- Google Wave, www.wave.google.com

- Zoho, www.zoho.com

Chat

Chat with text, audio, or video:

- Meebo, www.meebo.com
- Pidgin, www.pidgin.im
- Skype, www.skype.com
- Yahoo! Messenger, www.messenger.yahoo.com
- Tiny Chat, tinychat.com

Social Networks

Online communities where people can meet, converse, and share:

- Facebook, www.facebook.com
- LinkedIn, www.linkedin.com
- Ning, www.ning.com

Miscellaneous Tools and Resources

- Creative Commons, www.creativecommons.org
- TweetGrid, www.tweetgrid.com
- Twitter, www.twitter.com
- Widgetbox, www.widgetbox.com

Glossary

API. application programming interface. A part of a program that allows information from one program to be used in another program to create a new display of information.

Backchannel. A side conversation that occurs simultaneously online during a conference session, class, or other gathering.

Benevolent Dictator. Term used by Jeff Howe in his book *Crowdsourcing* that states that a successful mob should have a leader who guides, facilitates gently, and provides light-handed direction, while letting the group do most of the deciding and leading.

Cloud Computing. Using an offsite computer network to store data and run software; services of this kind are free or very cheap and allow users to have access to their content on any device with an internet connection.

Foobar. A placeholder name used in computer programming

GUI. graphical user interface. Interface with which the user can interact with the program by using a screen based on pictures and buttons instead of typing commands.

Hashtag. Tag used in Twitter that is a word or phrase preceded by a # symbol, as in *#mobrulelearning*.

The Law of Two Feet. Principle stating that people should be able to use their feet to vote for things that are the most engaging, get up and move away from things they find boring, and join discussions they find interesting.

Long Tail. Idea popularized by Chris Anderson in a *Wired* magazine article in 2004 and later in a book of the same title in 2006, the concept of niche marketing in which items that have low demand collectively have higher demand than a handful of popular items.

Open Creative Community. Term coined by Mark Kuznicki that strives to define the way some communities combine a passion for an interest or idea with creativity and an open door.

Open Space Technology. A meeting structure started by Harrison Owen in 1983 in which a group of people are given a purpose and freedom with little or no agenda, no predetermined outcomes, and no predetermined leaders can produce results.

Plug-in. Program that is created to "plug into" a larger program and adds functionality to the larger program.

Read/Write Web. Version of the internet that encourages—and is built by—active participation, creation, and community.

Remix Culture. Idea that everything is available to be made into something else; the culture of creation that takes part of an existing song, piece of art, or writing and adds something more and creates something new.

Third Place. Place where people find community outside of their home and work sphere.

Web 2.0. A participatory, user-oriented internet, made up of tools and applications that allow the web to be a place not only of community, but of creation.

Wikinomics. The economy of the mob; the mob will decide collectively what is valuable and true, be it information or items for sale.

ABOUT THE AUTHOR

Michelle Boule is a Geek Librarian living in Houston, Texas. Michelle went to Texas A&M University and received her MLS from Texas Woman's University. She was recently a social sciences librarian at the University of Houston. She now spends her time writing and consulting while trying to care for her growing brood of children and large dogs. In 2008, she was named a *Library Journal* Mover and Shaker. Michelle has created online learning environments, taught in-person classes, presented on a wide variety of technology and training subjects, shelved books, read books, written articles, organized unconferences, and participated in subversive activities in an effort to save the world. Michelle will read almost anything in book form, loves to cook, bake, go camping, and believes Joss Whedon is a genius. Michelle can be found online at A Wandering Eyre (www.wanderingeyre.com).

INDEX

Figures are indicated with "f."

A

Abram, Stephen, 192
abstract conceptualization, 105, 106, 107
active experimentation, 105, 106
active learners, 38, 106
advertising, 9, 43, 50–51
agenda planning
    Open Space Technology events, 19–20
    traditional conferences, 7, 9–10, 11, 12
    unconferences, 23, 35–36, 40–41, 51, 60–62, 69, 70f, 71
amateurs, 145–146
American Library Association (ALA), 12–13, 45, 79–84
Anderson, Chris, 14
Animoto, 128
APIs (application programming interfaces), 84
application of knowledge, 7, 8, 38, 106, 109, 167–168
appreciative inquiry, 27
archiving, information, 56, 57, 62–65
asynchronous events, 118
attendance, 55, 72, 115–116
attendees, 9–10, 19, 37. *See also* participants (unconferences)
autonomy, 168
Al-Azhar University, 100

B

backchannels
    benefits, 62
    definition, 8
    education case studies using, 181–182, 187
    learning process impacted by, 112, 121
    methods, 61–62
    technology requirements for, 42, 56
BarCamp, 38, 49, 71–73
Basecamp, 60
Baylor University, 189
Beale, Scott, 68
benevolent dictators, 25, 44–45, 198
Berlind, David, 84
BIGWIG (Blogs, Interactive Groupware Wikis Interest Group), 79–82, 81f

219

More Great Books from Information Today, Inc.

Dancing With Digital Natives
Staying in Step With the Generation That's Transforming the Way Business Is Done

Edited by Michelle Manafy and Heidi Gautschi

Generational differences have always influenced how business is done, but in the case of digital natives—those immersed in digital technology from birth—we are witnessing a tectonic shift. As an always connected, socially networked generation increasingly dominates business and society, organizations can ignore the implications only at the risk of irrelevance. In this fascinating book, Michelle Manafy, Heidi Gautschi, and a stellar assemblage of experts from business and academia provide vital insights into the characteristics of this transformative generation. Here is an in-depth look at how digital natives work, shop, play and learn, along with practical advice geared to help managers, marketers, coworkers, and educators maximize their interactions and create environments where everyone wins.

408 pp/hardbound/ISBN 978-0-910965-87-3 $27.95

Information Nation
Education and Careers in the Emerging Information Professions

By Jeffrey M. Stanton, Indira R. Guzman, and Kathryn R. Stam

Information and IT are central to virtually every industry in which the U.S. plays a leadership role. Here, three dedicated educators present research on students and workers in the information professions. They look at barriers to inclusion and retention, analyze the forces that prevent high school and college students from gaining needed interdisciplinary skills, and tell the stories of a diverse group of students who are thriving in new majors and new jobs.

256 pp/softbound/ISBN 978-1-57387-401-9 $35.00

The Internet Book of Life
Use the Web to Grow Richer, Smarter, Healthier, and Happier

By Irene E. McDermott

No matter what you want to accomplish in life, there are quality, free online resources available to help—if you only had the time to find and evaluate them all! Now, noted author, columnist, reference librarian, and working mom Irene McDermott rides to the rescue with *The Internet Book of Life*—a handy guide to websites, blogs, online tools, and mobile apps. From matters of personal finance to parenting, relationships, health and medicine, careers, travel, hobbies, pets, home improvement, and more, each chapter addresses real-life goals, dilemmas, and solutions. *The Internet Book of Life*—along with its supporting blog—is the lively, indispensable reference that belongs next to every home computer.

320 pp/softbound/ISBN 978-0-910965-89-7 $19.95

Research on Main Street
Using the Web to Find Local Business and Market Information

By Marcy Phelps

Even in a global economy, businesses need targeted, localized information about customers, companies, and industries. But as skilled searchers know, adding the element of geography to any research project creates new challenges. With *Research on Main Street*, Marcy Phelps presents a unique and useful guide to finding business and market information about places—including counties, cities, census blocks, and other sub-state areas—using free and low-cost online resources. You'll learn expert techniques and strategies for approaching location-specific research, including advice on how to tap local sources for in-depth information about business and economic conditions, issues, and outlooks. In addition to sharing her own well-honed expertise, Phelps incorporates a wealth of advice from her fellow business researchers throughout. Don't miss the author's companion website at www.ResearchOnMainStreet.com!

280 pp/softbound/ISBN 978-0-910965-88-0 $29.95

Teach Beyond Your Reach

An Instructor's Guide to Developing and Running Successful Distance Learning Classes, Workshops, Training Sessions and More

By Robin Neidorf

Distance learning is enabling individuals to earn college and graduate degrees, professional certificates, and a wide range of skills and credentials. In addition to the rapidly expanding role of distance learning in higher education, all types of organizations now offer web-based training courses to employees, clients, and other associates. In *Teach Beyond Your Reach,* teacher and author Robin Neidorf takes a practical, curriculum-focused approach designed to help new and experienced distance educators develop and deliver quality courses and training sessions. She shares best practices and examples, surveys the tools of the trade, and covers key issues, including instructional design, course craft, adult learning styles, student-teacher interaction, strategies for building a community of learners, and much more. Read this informative and inspiring book to master the evolving art and science of distance education.

248 pp/softbound/ISBN 978-0-910965-73-6 $29.95

The Extreme Searcher's Internet Handbook, 3rd Edition

A Guide for the Serious Searcher

By Randolph Hock

The Extreme Searcher's Internet Handbook is the essential guide for anyone who uses the internet for research—librarians, teachers, students, writers, business professionals, and others who need to search the web proficiently. In this fully updated third edition, Ran Hock covers strategies and tools for all major areas of internet content. Readers with little to moderate searching experience will appreciate Hock's helpful, easy-to-follow advice, while experienced searchers will discover a wealth of new ideas, techniques, and resources.

368 pp/softbound/ISBN 978-0-910965-84-2 $24.95

Web of Deceit
Misinformation and Manipulation in the Age of Social Media

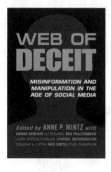

Edited by Anne P. Mintz

For all its amazing benefits, the worldwide social media phenomenon has provided manipulative people and organizations with the tools (and human targets) that allow hoaxes and con games to be perpetrated on a vast scale. In this eye-opening follow-up to her popular 2002 book, *Web of Deception*, Anne P. Mintz brings together a team of experts to explain how misinformation is intentionally spread and to illuminate the dangers in a range of critical areas. *Web of Deceit* is a must-read for any internet user who wants to avoid being victimized.

February 2012/320 pp/softbound/ISBN 978-0-910965-91-0 $29.95

The Mobile Marketing Handbook, 2nd Edition
A Step-by-Step Guide to Creating Dynamic Mobile Marketing Campaigns

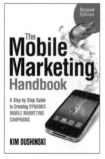

By Kim Dushinski

Mobile technology not only lets marketers reach customers where they are, it allows them to engage mobile users by targeting their immediate and specific needs. Giving users what they want when they want it is the unique value proposition of mobile marketing. In this fully updated second edition, mobile marketing consultant Kim Dushinski offers advice for firms that want to interact with mobile users, build stronger customer relationships, reach a virtually unlimited number of prospects, and gain competitive advantage by making the move to mobile now.

February 2012/224 pp/softbound/ISBN 978-0-910965-90-3 $29.95